C000048146

PENGUIN BOOKS

In Consolation to his Wife

Plutarch

c. 46 AD–120 AD

Plutarch

In Consolation to his Wife

TRANSLATED BY ROBIN WATERFIELD

PENGUIN BOOKS — GREAT IDEAS

PENGUIN BOOKS

Published by the Penguin Group
Penguin Books Ltd, 80 Strand, London WC2R ORL, England
Penguin Group (USA) Inc., 375 Hudson Street, New York, New York 10014, USA
Penguin Group (Canada), 90 Eglinton Avenue East, Suite 700, Toronto, Ontario, Canada M4P 2Y3
(a division of Pearson Penguin Canada Inc.)
Penguin Ireland, 25 St Stephen's Green, Dublin 2, Ireland (a division of Penguin Books Ltd)
Penguin Group (Australia), 250 Camberwell Road, Camberwell, Victoria 3124, Australia
(a division of Pearson Australia Group Pty Ltd)
Penguin Books India Pvt Ltd, 11 Community Centre, Panchsheel Park, New Delhi – 110 017, India
Penguin Group (NZ), 67 Apollo Drive, Rosedale, North Shore 0632, New Zealand
(a division of Pearson New Zealand Ltd)
Penguin Books (South Africa) (Pty) Ltd, 24 Sturdee Avenue, Rosebank, Johannesburg 2196, South Africa

Penguin Books Ltd, Registered Offices: 80 Strand, London WC2R ORL, England

www.penguin.com

Essays first published in this translation in Penguin Classic 1992
This selection first published 2008

2

Translation copyright © Robin Waterfield, 1992

All rights reserved

The moral right of the translator has been asserted

Set by Rowland Phototypesetting Ltd, Bury St Edmunds, Suffolk
Printed in England by Clays Ltd, St Ives plc

Except in the United States of America, this book is sold subject
to the condition that it shall not, by way of trade or otherwise, be lent,
re-sold, hired out, or otherwise circulated without the publisher's
prior consent in any form of binding or cover other than that in
which it is published and without a similar condition including this
condition being imposed on the subsequent purchaser

978-0-141-04252-7

www.greenpenguin.co.uk

Penguin Books is committed to a sustainable future
for our business, our readers and our planet.
The book in your hands is made from paper
certified by the Forest Stewardship Council.

Contents

In consolation to his wife

FROM PLUTARCH TO HIS WIFE. I hope this finds you well. The man you sent to give me the news of our child's death seems to have missed me during his overland journey to Athens, but I heard about it from my grand-daughter when I got to Tanagra. I imagine that the burial rites are over by now, and I hope they were conducted in a way that makes the chance of your feeling distress at the burial both now and in the future as remote as possible. But if there is something you haven't yet done, even though you want to, because you are waiting to hear what I intend to do, and it is something which you think would make things easier to bear, then it will happen too, with no fuss and superstitious nonsense – not that you are at all liable to these faults.

All I ask, my dear, is that while reacting emotionally you make sure that both of us – me as well as you – remain in a stable state. I mean, the actual event is a known quantity and I can keep it within limits, but if I find your distress excessive, this will discompose me more than what has happened. Nevertheless, I was not born 'from oak or rock', as you yourself know, given that you have been my partner in bringing up so many children – all brought up with no one else's help in our own home – and I know how overjoyed you were with the birth, after four sons, of the daughter you longed for and with the fact that it gave me the opportunity to name her after you. In addition, one's love for children of that age is peculiarly acute, since the pleasure it affords is absolutely unsullied and untainted by any element of anger and criticism. Also, she was inherently wonderfully easy to please and undemanding, and the way she repaid affection with affection and was so charming was not only delightful, but also made one realize how unselfish she was. She used to encourage her wet-nurse to offer and present her breast not only to other babies, but also to her favourite playthings and toys: she was unselfishly trying to share the good things she had and the things she most enjoyed with her favourites, as if they were guests at her very own table.

However, my dear, I fail to see any reason why, when this and similar behaviour pleased us during her life, it should upset and trouble us when we recall it now. I worry about the alternative, however – that we might consign the memory of her to oblivion along with our distress. This would be to act like Clymene, who said, 'I hate the curved cornel bow! I wish there were no gymnasia!': she was always nervous about recalling her son, and avoided doing so, because distress was its companion, and it is natural to avoid anything painful. No, our daughter was the sweetest thing in the world to hug and watch and listen to, and by the same token she must remain and live on in our thoughts, and bring not just more, but a great deal more pleasure than distress – if it is plausible to expect that the arguments we have often deployed on others will help us in our hour of need – and we must not slump in dejection or shut ourselves away and so pay for those pleasures with distress that vastly outweighs it.

People who were with you also tell me, with some surprise, that you haven't adopted mourning clothes, that you didn't make yourself or your maids follow any ugly or harrowing practices and that the para-phernalia of an expensive celebration was absent from the funeral – that instead everything was conducted with discretion and in silence, and with only the essen-tial accoutrements. It was no surprise to me, how-ever, that you who never tricked yourself out for the theatre or a public procession, and never saw any point in extravagance even where your pleasures were con-cerned, maintained unaffectedness and frugality in sad circumstances.

The point is that Bacchic rites are not the only cir-cumstances which require a decent woman to remain uncorrupted: she should equally assume that the insta-bility and emotional disturbance which grief entails call for self-control, which is not, as is popularly supposed, the enemy of affection and love, but of mental indul-gence. Affection is what we gratify by missing, valuing and remembering the dead, but the insatiable desire for grief – a desire which makes us wail and howl – is just as contemptible as hedonistic indulgence, despite the notion that it is forgivable because, although it may be contemptible, it is accompanied not by any pleasure gained from the desire, but rather by distress and pain. Could there be anything more absurd than banishing excesses of laughter and mirth, and yet allowing the floodgates of tears and lamentation, which spring from the same source as merriment, to open to their fullest extent? Or – as some husbands do – quarrelling with their wives about extravagant hair perfume and gaudy clothing, and yet submitting when they cut off their hair in mourning, dye their clothes black and adopt ugly postures when sitting and uncomfortable ones when reclining at table? Or – and this is the most irritating of all – resisting and restraining their wives if they punish their servants of either sex excessively and unfairly, and yet ignoring the vicious, harsh punishments they inflict upon themselves when they are under the influence of emotion and misfortunes which actually call for a relaxed and charitable attitude?

Our relationship, however, my dear, is such that there never has been any occasion for us to quarrel on the one score, and there never will be any occasion for us to quarrel on the other, I am sure. On the one hand, every philosopher who has spent time with us and got to know us has been impressed with the inextravagance of your clothing and make-up, and with the modesty of your lifestyle, and every one of our fellow citizens has witnessed your unaffectedness during rituals and sacrifices and at the theatre. On the other hand, you have already demonstrated in the past that you can remain stable under these circumstances, when you lost your eldest child and again when our lovely Charon left us before his time. I remember that I brought visitors with me on my journey from the coast at the news of the child's death, and that they and everyone else gathered in our house. As they subsequently told others as well, when they saw how calm and peaceful it was, they thought that nothing terrible had happened and that a baseless rumour had got out, because you had behaved so responsibly in arranging the house at a time when disarray is normally excusable, despite the fact that you had nursed him at your own breast and had endured an operation when your nipple got inflamed, which are noble acts stemming from motherly love.

It is noticeable that most mothers take their children into their arms as if they were playthings (after others have cleaned them and smartened them up), and then, if the children die, these mothers wallow in empty, indecent grief. They are not motivated by warmth of feeling, which is a reasonable and commendable emotion: their strong inclination towards shallow beliefs, plus a dash of instinctive emotion, causes outbursts of grief which are fierce, manic and unruly. Aesop was apparently aware of this: he said that when Zeus was distributing recognition among the gods, Grief asked for some as well; so Zeus allowed Grief to be acknowledged – but only by people who deliberately wanted to acknowledge it.

This is certainly what happens at the beginning: only an individual lets grief enter himself; but after a while it becomes a permanent sibling, a habitual presence, and then it doesn't leave however much one wants it to. That is why it is crucial to resist it on the threshold and not to adopt special clothing or haircuts or anything else like that, which allow it to establish a stronghold. These things challenge the mind day in and day out, make it recoil, belittle it and constrict it and imprison it, and make it unresponsive and apprehensive, as if the wearing of these clothes and the adoption of these practices out of grief cut it off from laughter and light and the sociability of the table. The consequences of this affliction are physical neglect and an aversion to oiling and bathing the body and to other aspects of the daily regimen, when exactly the opposite should happen: purely mental suffering ought to be helped by physical fitness. Mental distress abates and subsides to a great extent when it is dispersed in physical calm, as waves subside in fair weather, but if as a result of a bad regimen the body becomes sordid and foul and transmits to the mind nothing benign or beneficial, but only the harsh and unpleasant fumes of pain and distress, then even those who desire it find that recovery becomes hard to achieve. These are the kinds of disorders that take possession of the mind when it is treated so badly.

Nevertheless, I have no cause to worry about the worst and most worrying disorder which occurs in such cases – 'the invasion of malignant women', with the cries and expressions of sympathy which they use to polish and hone distress, and to prevent its being diminished either by external factors or of its own accord. For I know about the battles you recently had when you went to assist Theon's sister and defended her against the incursions of the women who came with their weeping and wailing – behaviour which is exactly the same as fighting fire with fire. I mean, when people see a friend's house on fire, then everyone contributes what he can to put it out as quickly as possible; but when that same friend's mind is on fire, they bring fuel! And although when someone has an eye infection, people don't let just anyone touch it or treat the inflammation, people who are grieving sit and let everyone who comes by prod at their running sore, so to speak, and aggravate the condition, until instead of being an insignificant itching irritation, it erupts into a seriously disagreeable affliction. Anyway, I know that you will be on your guard against this.

Please try, however, to use your mind as a vehicle for often returning to the time when this child of ours had not yet been born and we had no reason to blame fortune; and then connect that time with the present, and imagine that our circumstances are no different again. You see, my dear, we will seem to regret that our child was ever born if we find more to complain about now than in the situation before her birth. We must not erase the intervening two years from our memories, but since they brought happiness and joy, we must count them as pleasant. The good was brief, but should not therefore be regarded as a long-term bad influence; and we should not be ungrateful for what we received just because our further hopes were dashed by fortune.

The point is that a reverential attitude towards the gods and being charitable and uncomplaining with regard to fortune always yield a dividend which is both fine and enjoyable, and anyone who, in a situation like ours, makes a particular point of highlighting the memory of good things and turning his mind away from the dark and disturbing aspects of his life towards the bright and brilliant ones instead either completely extinguishes whatever it is that is causing him pain, or at least decreases and obscures it by blending it with its opposite.

Perfume is always nice to smell, but it is also an antidote to unpleasant odours; likewise, bearing good things in mind serves the extra purpose of essential support, in times of trouble, for people who are not afraid to recall good times and do not critically hold fortune entirely responsible for every bad thing that happens. And that is a condition we should avoid – the syndrome of whingeing if the book of our life has a single smudge while every other page is perfectly clean. I mean, you have often been told that happiness is a consequence of correctly using the rational mind for the goal of a stable state, and that if it is a chance event which causes one to deviate, this does not constitute a major reversal and does not mean that the edifice of one's life has collapsed and been demolished.

Suppose that we too were to follow the usual practice of being guided by external circumstances, of keeping a tally of events due to fortune and of relying on any casual assessment of whether or not we are happy: even so, you should not take into consideration the current weeping and wailing of your visitors, which is trotted out on each and every occasion, prompted by pointless social customs. You would be better off bearing in mind that they continue to envy you for your children, your home and your way of life. As long as there are others who would gladly choose your fate, even including our present upset, it is awful for you, as the bearer of the fate, to complain and grumble, instead of letting the very source of your pain bring you to the realization of how much we have to be grateful for in what we still have. Otherwise, you will resemble those people who pick out

Homer's headless and tapering lines, and ignore the many extensive passages of outstanding composition: if you do this, and nitpickingly whinge about the bad features of your life, and gloss over the good points in a vague and sweeping fashion, you will be behaving like those mean and avaricious people who build up a considerable hoard and don't make use of what they get, but still moan and grumble when they lose it.

If you feel sorry about our daughter dying before she was able to marry and have children, then again you can find other reasons for cheering yourself up, in that you have known and experienced both these states: I mean, they cannot simultaneously be significant and insignificant blessings, depending on whether or not one has been deprived of them! And the fact that she has gone to a place of no pain ought not to be a source of pain to us. Why should she cause us to suffer, if there is nothing that can now cause her pain? Even huge losses cease to be a source of distress when the point is reached at which the objects are no longer missed, and your Timoxena suffered only minor losses, since what she was familiar with and what she found pleasure in were not things of great importance. And as for things she was unaware of, which had never entered her mind or caught her fancy – how could she be said to have lost them?

Then there is that other idea you've come across, which is commonly accepted, that it is quite impossible for anything to harm or distress something which has been dissolved. But I know that both the doctrine we've inherited from our ancestors and the maxims of the Dionysian Mysteries (which those of us who are in the group are privy to) prevent you believing this idea. So, since the soul cannot be destroyed, you can compare what happens to it to the behaviour of caged birds: if it has made a physical body its home for an extended period of time, and has allowed a plethora of material events and long familiarity to domesticate it to this way of life, then it resumes its perch inside a body and doesn't let go or stop its involvement, through rebirth after rebirth, with worldly conditions and fortunes. If old age is the butt of calumny and slurs, you should appreciate that this is not because of wrinkles, grey hair and physical enfeeblement: no, its most cruel feature is that it makes the soul lose touch with its memories of the other world, attaches it to this one, wraps and constricts it (since it retains the shape it gained while it was acted on by the body). On the other hand, a soul which, although captured, <remains only a short while in a body before being released> by the gods and departing, springs back up to its natural state as if, although it had been bent, it retained its suppleness and malleability. Just as fire is quickly rekindled again and returns to its former state if it is relit straight after being extinguished, <but the longer the interval, the harder it is to relight, so too the most fortunate soul is the one which is able, in the poet's words,> 'to pass as swiftly as possible through Hades' portals', before a strong love of the things of this world has been engendered in it and before it has become moulded to the body by being softened and melted as if by chemicals.

Our ancient ancestral customs and rules are a better guide to the truth in these matters. People do not pour

libations for their infant children when they die or perform any of the other rites that in other cases one is
expected to perform for the dead, because babies have
not been pervaded by earth or any earthly things. Again,
people do not linger over their burial or at their grave
or in laying out their bodies, because the laws regarding
death at that age do not allow it, on the grounds that it
is irreligious to grieve for those who have exchanged
this world for a fate, and a place too, that is better
and more divine. Since mistrusting these laws is more
problematic than trusting them, let us make sure that
our external actions conform to their injunctions, and
that our internal state is even more untainted, pure and
restrained than our external activity.

On being aware of moral progress

Is there any argument, Sosius Senecio, which will salvage one's sense that one is improving and approaching virtue, if in fact progress causes no relief from folly, but vice circumscribes every stage and exactly counterbalances the progress and 'drags it down as lead does a fishing-net'? Take, for example, music or literacy: there can be no recognition of improvement here either, if the lessons do nothing to whittle away one's ignorance of these subjects, and one's incompetence remains perpetually at a constant level. And if medical treatment fails to relieve a patient's discomfort or in some way alleviate the illness and cause its remission and decrease, then it cannot afford the patient any sense that his condition is changing for the better, until his body has completely recovered its strength and the treatment has engendered the opposite condition with no trace of illness at all.

In fact, however, people do not make progress in these domains unless they perceive the change, since the instrument of their progress is relief from what was weighing them down (as if they were on a balance, and were being carried upwards as opposed to their former downward movement). And likewise, in philosophy, no progress or awareness of progress can be assumed if the mind is not freeing and purifying itself of fallibility, but is involved in absolute vice right up to the moment when it secures absolute, perfect virtue. Of course, it takes only a moment, a split second, for the wise man to change from the worst possible iniquity to a state of consummate virtue! And in an instant he has totally and utterly escaped from the vice which he did not even partially eliminate over a lengthy period!

Still, I am sure you already know that the authors of *these* assertions turn out to find 'the wise man who is unaware' extremely awkward and problematic, thanks to their own assertions. Consider a person who has not yet grasped the fact that he has become wise, but is unaware and uncertain in this regard, because it has escaped his notice that, by a gradual and lengthy process of subtracting this and adding that, progress has taken place and has steadily led him, as if it were a road, to an appointment with virtue. But if the speed and size of the change were so great that someone who is the worst of sinners in the morning can become a perfect saint in the evening, or if change occurred in such a way that someone could go to bed worthless and wake up wise and, with his mind freed of yesterday's fallibility and liability to error, could say, 'Goodbye, false dreams; I now see that you were nothing – if all this were so, how could anyone not realize that a change of this magnitude had happened within himself and that wisdom had enlightened him all at once? I would sooner believe that someone like Caeneus, whose prayer to change sex from female to male is granted, could fail to notice the transformation, than that someone who had become controlled, wise and courageous instead of cowardly, stupid and weak-willed, and who has in an instant exchanged a life at a bestial level for one at the level of the gods, could be unaware of himself.

No, it is a correct saying that one should 'Fit the stone to the line, not the line to the stone.' But the people who refuse to fit their views to the facts, and instead force facts into unnatural conformity with their hypotheses, have infected philosophy with plenty of puzzles: the one which fits everyone, with the sole exception of the perfect man, into a single undifferentiated category of vice is only the greatest of these puzzles. This puzzle makes the term 'progress' opaque: what they call 'progress' is a state little short of sheer inanity, and a state which makes all those who have not rid themselves of every emotion and defect still just as miserably off as those who have not escaped even any of the very worst vices. Anyway, these thinkers refute themselves, because in their lectures they place Aristides on a par with Phalaris in respect of immorality, and Brasidas with Dolon in respect of cowardice, and even go so far as to claim that Plato and Meletus are utterly identical in respect of ignorance; but in their lives and actions they refrain and abstain from the behaviour of the latter set of people, which they acknowledge to be heartless, and attach themselves to and trust the former set, whose example, as they agree, is in the most important respects of great value.

We, on the other hand, can see that 'more and less' can be attributed to every kind of vice, and especially to mental vice, which is a genus comprising an indeterminate, limitless number of species; and we can see that this is also what makes different stages of progress different, as reason gradually illuminates and purifies the mind by pushing back imperfection as if it were darkness. Consequently, we do not find illogical the notion that people who are being carried upwards out of an abyss, so to speak, are aware of the change, and we think that this awareness has definite, describable principles.

Here, without further ado, is the first such principle to consider. Just as those who are running under sail in the open sea use the time along with the strength of the wind to calculate how much of their voyage they are likely to have accomplished, given that x amount of time has passed and they are being driven by y amount of power, so in philosophy one can, to satisfy oneself, take as evidence of progress the continuity and constancy of the journey, and the fact that it is rarely interrupted by pauses followed by fresh effort and impetus, but is perpetually pressing forward smoothly and evenly, and using reason to secure its passage without stumbling. The advice 'If you add even a small amount to a small amount and do this often' is valuable for more than just the accumulation of money: it is universally effective, and nowhere more so than in the development of virtue, when to reason is added plenty of habituation, which is what produces results.

Any unevenness and dullness, however, on the part of philosophers makes them not only wait and linger on the journey of progress, so to speak, but even turn back, because vice seizes every opportunity to ambush anyone who gives in and takes time off, and to carry him away in the opposite direction. Mathematicians tell us that when the planets stop moving forwards, they become stationary, but in philosophy, when progress ceases, there is no gap, no stationary mode. Since human nature is constantly in motion, it tends to tilt as if it were on a pair of scales: it is either fully extended by its better movements or, thanks to the opposite movements, it plummets towards its worse aspect. So if – as in the oracle uttered by the god which stated, 'Fight against the Cirrhaeans every day and every night' – if you are aware of having resisted vice day in and day out without stopping, or at least of having rarely let down your guard or of having only occasionally admitted into your presence certain pleasures or amusements or diversions with a view to making a deal with them, as if they were envoys from the army of vice, then you have every reason to proceed towards the future undaunted and in good heart.

Nevertheless, even if breaks occur in one's philosophical activity, if later there is more stability to it and longer stretches of time are spent on it than before, then this is a good indication that hard work and repeated effort are squeezing laziness out. The other alternative, however, is bad – when after a short while setbacks frequently and continually occur, with enthusiasm shrivelling, so to speak. A reed starts growing with a huge spurt whose result is a smooth, unbroken length, and at first it is rarely thwarted or retarded and only at long intervals; but then (as if it had difficulty breathing up there) it grows weak and consequently starts to fail and its growth is hampered by the formation of many protuberances, with little room between them, as its life-force encounters bumps and shocks. This is an analogy for what can happen in philosophy: anyone who starts with a series of energetic charges, and then continually encounters drawbacks and interruptions in large numbers, while seeing no improvement, gets fed up and gives in. 'On the other hand, he gains wings' applies to anyone who is motivated by the benefit of philosophy and who, with strength and enthusiasm generated by achievement, cuts through the excuses as if they were a crowd of nuisances.

When you are with someone you find attractive, it is not happiness that is a sign of falling in love (since this is not unique to love), but pain and distress when you are cut off from that person; and likewise, plenty of people are drawn to philosophy and apparently set about learning with a great deal of zeal, if nothing else, but if other matters or diversions drive them away, that emotion drains out of them and their mood becomes one of indifference. On the other hand, 'anyone smitten by love for his beloved' might strike you as placid and tame while you are together, sharing in philosophical discussion, but you should see him when he has been cut off and separated from philosophy: he is feverish, restless, dissatisfied with every matter and every diversion; his longing for philosophy impels him, as though he were a mindless beast, to forget his friends. The point is that what is required is not that people treat discussions as they do perfumes and enjoy them when they are there, but do not go out of their way for them, or even have a positive distaste for them, when they are not there; what is important is rather that, when one is cut off from philosophical discussions (whether it is getting married or a sea journey or forming a friendship or military service that causes the separation), one should feel something similar to hunger and thirst, and so stay in contact with the genuine cause of progress. For the greater the gain from philosophy has been, the greater the displeasure at separation.

What we have been saying is basically identical or very similar to the ancient description of progress in Hesiod – that the path ceases being steep or excessively sheer: it becomes easy, level and manageable. It is as if repeated effort levels the path, and as though the journey creates a light and a brightness in philosophy, to replace the perplexity, uncertainty and vacillation which students of philosophy come across at first, like sailors who have left the land they know, but cannot yet see the land which is their destination. For they are in the position of having left behind what is normal and familiar, but of having not yet become acquainted with and in possession of what is better: they are going round in circles in the intermediate area, and in the process often turn back towards where they have come from.

Sextius the Roman was a case in point: the story goes that on account of philosophy he had abandoned his offices and positions of authority in the political arena, but on the other hand was, while in the philosophical arena, in a bad way and was finding the subject difficult; he came very close to throwing himself off the top of a building. And there is a similar story about Diogenes of Sinope when he was embarking on his study of philosophy: it was an Athenian holiday, and they were having fun and staying awake all night, with meals laid on by the state, plays at the theatres, and parties with one another; Diogenes was curled up in a corner of the agora, trying to sleep, and he found himself thinking decidedly upsetting and self-destructive thoughts, trying to work out how, under no external compulsion, he had of his own free will taken on a gruelling and unnatural lifestyle, and was sitting there excluded from all those good things. Just then, however (as the story goes), a mouse crept up and occupied itself with the crumbs from his bread; Diogenes started to use his mind and reconsider, and said to himself, in a critical and disparaging tone, 'What are you getting at, Diogenes? Your leftovers are a feast for this mouse, yet you, a man of stature – are you complaining and moaning just because you're not lying over there on soft, gaudy blankets, getting drunk?' So when that sort of bad mood occurs only rarely, and the mind quickly steps in to cancel it out and repel it (changing defeat into victory, as it were), and has no difficulty in getting rid of the agitation and restlessness, then one ought to regard one's progress as being on a firm basis.

Their own weakness, however, is not the only factor which can make students of philosophy waver and double back. The earnest advice of friends and the mocking, bantering attacks of critics can also, on their occurrence, warp and sap resolve, and have been known to put some people off philosophy altogether. Therefore, a good indication of an individual's progress would be equanimity when faced with these factors, and not being upset or irritated by people who name his peers and tell him how they are prospering at some royal household, or are marrying into money or are going down to the agora as the people's choice for some political or forensic post. For anyone who is not dismayed or swayed in these circumstances has clearly been suitably and securely gripped by philosophy, since it is impossible to stop trying to conform to behaviour the majority of people admire unless one has become accustomed to admire virtue instead; even anger and insanity give some people the ability to stand up to others, but disdain for affairs commonly admired is impossible without a high purpose, truly and securely held.

This is also the context of the proud comparisons people make between the two concerns, as when Solon said, 'We will not exchange our virtue for their wealth, since the one is permanent and stable, but different people have money at different times.' And Diogenes used to compare his moves from Corinth to Athens and back again to the great king's residency at Susa in the spring, at Babylon in the winter and in Media in the summer. Then there is Agesilaus' remark about the great king: 'He is a greater man than me only if he is more moral.' And in a letter to Antipater about Alexander, Aristotle wrote that the fact that Alexander rules over a lot of people does not make him the only one who can legitimately feel proud: anyone whose thinking about the gods is correct has just as much right. And when Zeno saw that Theophrastus was admired for the number of his students, he said, 'Although his chorus is larger, mine is more harmonious.' Anyway, when the contrast between virtue and externals has enabled you to eliminate from yourself envy and jealousy of others, and all the things which commonly irritate and undermine beginners in philosophy, you can take this too as a clear indication of your progress.

Another not unimportant sign is a certain change where arguments are concerned. Almost without exception, beginners in philosophy tend to look for ways of speaking which will enhance their reputation. Some behave like birds: because they are lightweight and ambitious, they swoop down on to the brilliant heights of science. Others behave 'like puppies', as Plato says: 'they enjoy dragging things around and tearing them apart', so they head for controversies and puzzles and sophisms. A great many beginners immerse themselves in philosophical arguments and use them as ammunition in casuistry. Occasionally, beginners go around collecting quotable phrases and stories, but just as Anacharsis used to say that, in his experience, the only reason the Greeks have money is to count it, so these people – in respect of the arguments they employ – are short-changed and short-change others, and accumulate nothing else which might do them good.

The result of all this is illustrated by Antiphanes' saying, in its application to Plato's circle. Antiphanes used to tell an amusing story about a city where, as soon as anyone spoke, the sound of his voice was frozen solid, and then later, when it thawed out in the summer, they heard what had been said in the winter; likewise, he added, what Plato said to people when they were still young only just got through to most of them much later, when they were old. People also have this experience when faced with philosophy in any form, and it stops only when their discrimination becomes sound and steady, and begins to encounter the factors which instil moral character and stature, and starts to seek out arguments whose tracks (to borrow Aesop's image) tend inwards rather than outwards. Sophocles used to say that he first lightened Aeschylus' heaviness, then the austerity and affectedness of his own style, and only then did he, as a third step, try to change the actual nature of the language, which has the most bearing on morality and virtue; this is an analogy for the fact that it is only when students of philosophy stop using arguments for display and affectedness and turn to the kinds of argument which have an impact on the character and the emotions that they begin to make genuine, unassuming progress.

In the first place, then, you must make sure that when you are reading philosophical works and listening to philosophical lectures, you do not concentrate on the phraseology and exclude the subject-matter, and that you do not pounce on awkward, odd phrases rather than those which are useful, meaty and beneficial. Secondly, you must be careful, when you spend time on poetry and history, in case you overlook any well-expressed point which might improve your character or ease the weight of your emotions. For just as a bee spends time with flowers, as Simonides says, 'intent on yellow honey', whereas everyone else appreciates and takes in no more of the flower than its colour and scent, so, although everyone else's involvement with poetry has the limited aim of pleasure and fun, nevertheless if someone by his own resources discovers and gathers from it something worth taking seriously, then it is by this token plausible to suggest that his training and love for what is good and congruent with his nature have brought him to the point of recognizing what is good and congruent.

There are people, for example, whose concern with Plato and Xenophon is limited to their language, and who glean no more than their pure Attic diction (which is, as it were, the dew and down on the flower). The only comment one can make about such people is that they appreciate the nice, flowery smell of medicines, but fail to ingest, or even recognize, their analgesic and purgative properties. By contrast, those whose progress is ongoing are capable of benefiting, and of gathering what is congruent and useful, not just from the written or spoken word, but from any sight and any situation at all.

Anecdotes about Aeschylus and others of similar stature illustrate the point. For instance, Aeschylus was watching a boxing-match at the Isthmian games, and whenever either of the boxers was struck, the audience yelled out loud; Aeschylus nudged Ion of Chios and said, 'Do you see what practice can do? The man who has been struck remains quiet – it is the spectators who cry out!' Brasidas once picked up some dried figs which had a mouse among them; the mouse nipped him and he dropped it: 'Incredible!' he remarked. 'No matter how small or weak a creature is, it will live if it has the courage to defend itself.' When Diogenes saw someone using his hands to drink, he took his cup out of his bag and threw it away.

These stories illustrate how attention and repeated intense effort enable people to notice and absorb the implicit virtue in everything. This is more likely to happen if they supplement theory with practice – not just 'by studying in the school of danger', as Thucydides puts it, but also by giving themselves a practical demonstration of their views – or preferably, forming their views by experience – whenever they are faced with pleasure and argumentativeness, or involved in decision-making, advocacy in court and political authority. As for those who, even while they are still students, occupy themselves with considering what they can take from philosophy and recycle without delay in the political arena, or to entertain their young friends, or at a reception given by the king, they are no more entitled to be regarded as philosophers than sellers of medicines are entitled to be regarded as doctors; or perhaps a better description is to say that a sophist of this kind is basically altogether identical to Homer's bird, because he regurgitates for his pupils, as if they were his 'flightless chicks', anything he takes in, 'and fares badly himself', if he fails to consider his own advantage and to absorb or digest anything he takes in.

It is therefore essential for us to make sure, first, that we approach words in a way that is beneficial to ourselves, and second, where other people are concerned, that we do so not because we want empty glory or public recognition, but rather because we want to be taught and to teach. Above all, we must make sure that, when investigating issues, there is no trace of rivalry and contentiousness, and that we have stopped supplying ourselves with arguments as if they were boxing thongs or padded gloves to be used against one another, and no longer prefer bludgeoning others to the ground to learning and teaching. Reasonableness and civility during discussions, neither embarking on conversations competitively nor ending them in anger, neither crowing if an argument is won nor sulking if it is lost – all this is the behaviour of someone who is progressing nicely. Aristippus gives us an example: once he was outmanoeuvred in an argument by a man who did not lack self-confidence, only intelligence and sense; Aristippus saw that the man was delighted and had got big-headed, so he said, 'I am going home now: I may have been argued down by you, but I will sleep more peacefully tonight than you, for all your success.'

When we speak, we can also assess ourselves by seeing whether or not we get afraid and hold back if a large crowd unexpectedly gathers round us, whether or not we get depressed if there are only a few to hear us debate, and whether or not, if called upon to address the Assembly or a person in authority, we throw the opportunity away by being inadequately prepared with respect to what language to use. This latter point is illustrated by stories about Demosthenes and Alcibiades. Alcibiades was extremely adept at knowing what topics to address, but less confident about what language to use and, as a result, used to trip himself up while he was addressing topics; often, even in the middle of speaking, he used to search for and hunt after an elusive word or phrase, and so get booed. By contrast, Homer was not bothered about publishing an unmetrical first line: his talent gave him plenty of self-assurance about the rest of the poem. It is therefore fairly reasonable to suppose that those who are striving for virtue and goodness will make good use of the opportunity and the topic, by being completely indifferent to any tumultuous, noisy response to their language.

The same applies to actions as well as to words: everyone should try to ensure that they contain more usefulness than showmanship, and are more concerned with truth than with display. If genuine love for a young man or for a woman does not seek witnesses, but reaps its harvest of pleasure even if it fulfils its desire in secret, then it is even more likely that someone who loves goodness and wisdom, who is intimate and involved with virtue because of his actions, will be quietly self-assured within himself, and will have no need of an admiring audience. There was a man who summoned his serving-woman at home and shouted out, 'Look at me, Dionysia: I have stopped being big-headed!' Analogous to this is the behaviour of someone who politely does a favour and then runs around telling everyone about it: it is obvious that he is still dependent on external appreciation and drawn towards public recognition, that he does not yet have virtue in his sights and that he is not awake, but is acting randomly among the illusory shadows of a dream and then presents his action for viewing, as if it were a painting.

It follows that giving something to a friend and doing a favour for an acquaintance, but not telling others about it, is a sign of progress. And voting honestly when surrounded by corruption, rejecting a dishonourable petition from an affluent or powerful person, spurning bribes and even not drinking when thirsty at night or resisting a kiss from a good-looking woman or man, as Agesilaus did – quietly keeping any of these to oneself is also a sign of progress. A man like this gains recognition from himself, and he feels not contempt, but pleasure and contentment at being self-sufficient as a witness, and spectator too, of his good deeds; this shows that reason is now being nourished within and is taking root inside him, and that he 'is getting used to being his own source of pleasure', as Democritus puts it.

Farmers prefer to see ears of corn bent over, nodding towards the ground; they regard as worthless impostors the light ones which stand up straight. Young would-be philosophers are just the same: it is those who are particularly insubstantial and lightweight who cut a dash, pose and strut, faces full of contempt and disdain which spare nothing and nobody; but when they start to fill out and gain in yield from the lectures, they shed their ostentatious pomposity. And just as the air inside empty vessels into which liquid is introduced is squeezed out and goes elsewhere, so when people are filled with genuinely good material, their pretensions are pushed aside and their self-esteem starts to crumble; they stop feeling proud of their beard and threadbare gown, and instead make their minds the object of their efforts; and they use the caustic, harsh side of their nature on themselves above all, and treat anyone else they come across with greater leniency. They put an end to their former habit of usurping and confiscating for themselves the name of philosophy and the reputation of studying philosophy; instead, if an innately good young man is even called 'philosopher' by someone else, he will be so dismayed that he will say with a smile, overcome by embarrassment, 'Look, I am no god. Why do you compare me to the gods?' As Aeschylus says, 'When a young woman has experienced a man, the heat in her eyes gives her away'; and when a young man has experienced genuine philosophical progress, these lines of Sappho's are relevant: 'I am tongue-tied, and delicate fire plays over my skin' – despite which, his gaze is unworried and his eye calm and you would want to hear him speak.

At the start of the initiation ceremony, as the candidates assemble, they are noisy, call out and jostle one another; but when the rituals are being performed and revealed, then they pay attention in awestruck silence. Likewise, you can see plenty of disturbance and chatter and self-assurance at the beginning of philosophy, on the threshold, with some people rudely and roughly jostling for acclamation; but anyone who finds himself inside and in the presence of a great light, with the sanctuary open, so to speak, changes his attitude and becomes quiet and transfixed, and 'with humility and restraint complies' with reason, as he would with a god. Menedemus' joke seems to apply rather neatly to such people. He said that the numerous people who sail to Athens to study go through the following progression: they start wise, then become philosophers, and as time goes on, they become normal people, by gradually laying aside their self-esteem and pretensions in proportion to the hold they have on reason.

When people need healing, if it is a tooth or a finger that is hurting, they go straight to the doctor; if they have a fever, they summon the doctor to their house and ask him to help; but if they are suffering from an extreme case – melancholy or brain fever or delirium – they sometimes cannot even stand the doctor coming to visit them, but chase him away or avoid him, because the severity of their illness prevents them even being aware that they are ill. The same goes for people with faults: it is the incurable ones who get angry and behave aggressively and fiercely towards anyone who tries to rebuke and reprimand them, whereas those who put up with rebuke and do not resist are in a more composed state. And when someone with faults puts himself in the hands of critics, talks about his defects, does not hide his iniquity and does not relish getting away with it or enjoy being unrecognized for what he is, but admits it and begs for someone to take him and reprimand him, this must be a significant sign of progress. This is surely why Diogenes used to say that anyone concerned about safety ought to try to find either a proper friend or a fervent enemy, so that one way or another – either by being rebuked or by being treated – he might steer clear of badness.

Imagine someone with an obvious stain or mark on his clothes or a torn shoe affecting self-deprecation as a pretence to the outside world, or someone thinking that by making fun of his own short stature or slumped posture he is showing a carefree spirit: as long as he does all this, but disguises the internal blemishes of his mind, the defects of his life, the pettiness, hedonism, malice and spite, and hides them away as if they were boils, without letting anyone touch them or see them because he is afraid of being rebuked, then his involvement in progress is minimal, or rather non-existent. On the other hand, anyone who comes to grips with these defects, and primarily anyone who has the ability and the desire to supply his own distress at and censure for his faults, but secondly anyone who has the ability and the desire to put himself in someone else's hands for castigation, and sticks with it, and is purified by the criticism, is precisely the person who seems to have a genuine loathing for iniquity, and to be really trying to eradicate it.

It is, of course, important to feel embarrassed at, and to avoid, even a reputation for badness; but someone who dislikes actual iniquity more than he dislikes an adverse reputation does not avoid being reproached, and reproaching others himself, if the object is moral improvement. For instance, there is Diogenes' nice remark to a young man he saw in a pub, who ran away – but into the pub: 'The further inside you run,' he said, 'the more you are going to be in the pub!' And the more a person denies any defect, the more he immerses and imprisons himself in the vice. It is obvious that anyone who is poor, but who pretends to be rich, increases his poverty by his masquerade; but Hippocrates, who wrote down and published the fact that he did not understand the skull's sutures, is a model for anyone who is genuinely progressing, because he thinks it quite wrong for Hippocrates to help others avoid the situation he found himself in by publicizing his own failing, while he – a person who is committed to immunity from error – does not dare to be castigated or to admit his fallibility and ignorance.

In fact, it is arguable that Bion's and Pyrrho's assertions refer not to progress, but to a better, more perfect state. Bion told his friends that they deserved to think they were progressing when they could listen to abuse and be affected as if what was being said was 'My friend, you don't seem bad or foolish, so I wish you health and great joy, and may the gods grant you prosperity.' And there is a story about Pyrrho that once when he was endangered by a storm at sea, he pointed to a piglet which was happily tucking into some barley that had been spilled, and told his companions that anyone who did not want to be disturbed by events should use the rational mind and philosophy to develop a similar detachment.

You should also notice what Zeno said – that a person's dreams ought to make him aware that he is progressing, if when asleep he sees himself neither enjoying anything discreditable, nor conniving at or doing anything awful or outrageous, but if instead he feels as though he were in translucent depths of tranquil stillness and it dawns upon him that the imaginative and emotional part of his mind has been dispersed by reason. Plato also apparently realized this point, before Zeno, and he described in outline the imaginative, irrational aspect of an innately tyrannical mind and the sorts of things it does when asleep: 'He tries to have sex with his mother', feels compulsions for all kinds of foods, transgresses convention and acts as though his desires, which by day are shamed and cowed into restraint by convention, had been set free.

Draught-animals which have been well trained do not attempt to stray and deviate, even if their master lets the reins go slack: they press forward in an orderly fashion, obedient to their conditioning, and unfailingly keep to their course. In the same way, people whose irrational aspect has been tamed and civilized and checked by reason find that it loses its readiness to use its desires to act outrageously and unconventionally even when dreaming or when under the influence of illness; instead, it watches protectively over its conditioning and remains aware of it, since it is conditioning which gives our attention strength and energy. If, as a result of training, detachment can gain control over even the body – over the whole body and any of its parts – so that eyes faced with a harrowing sight resist weeping and a heart surrounded by horrors resists lurching, and genitals modestly keep still and cause no trouble at all in the company of attractive men or women, then naturally this increases the plausibility of suggesting that training can take hold of the emotional part of the mind and, so to speak, smooth it and regularize it by suppressing its illusions and impressions at all levels, including dreaming.

There is a story about the philosopher Stilpo which illustrates the point. Once he dreamed he saw Poseidon and that Poseidon was angry with him for having omitted to sacrifice an ox (which was a standard offering to Poseidon), but Stilpo was not perturbed in the slightest and said, 'What do you mean, Poseidon? Don't you think it's childish of you to come and complain that I didn't bankrupt myself and fill the city with the smell of burnt offerings, but instead sacrificed to you on a moderate scale at home, drawing on what I actually had?' And then he dreamed that Poseidon smiled, extended his right hand and said that, because of Stilpo, he would create for Megara a bumper crop of sardines.

So anyway, when people have dreams which are pleasant, clear and untroubled, and sleep which brings back no trace of anything frightening or horrible, or malicious or warped, they say that these features are beams of the light of progress; but they say that the features of distressing and bizarre dreams – frenzy, agitation, running from danger like a coward, experiencing childish delights and miseries – are like breakers and billows, and originate in a mind which does not yet have its own regulator, but is still being formed by opinions and rules, so that when it is asleep and as far from these formative influences as it can be, it is again dissolved and unravelled by the emotions. Now, you must join me in considering, by yourself, whether this phenomenon I have been talking about stems from progress or from a state which already has the steady, solid strength which comes of being based on reason.

Since absolute detachment is an exalted, divine state, and progress towards it is, as I say, like a kind of alleviation and taming of the emotions, then it is important for us to examine our emotions and to assess their differences, comparing them with themselves and with one another. We must compare them with themselves to see if the desires and fears and rages we now experience are less intense than they were before, given that we are using reason rapidly to extinguish their violence and heat; and we must compare them with one another to see if our sense of disgrace is now more acute than our fear, and whether we prefer to emulate people rather than envy them, and value a good reputation more than we value money. In short, we must compare them with one another to see if, to use a musical analogy, we err on the side of the Dorian rather than the Lydian mode, whether our lifestyle inclines towards asceticism rather than indulgence, whether our actions tend to be slow rather than hasty, and whether we are astounded by rather than contemptuous of arguments and people. Where ailments are concerned, it is a good sign when the disease is diverted into parts of the body where it will not prove fatal; and likewise where vice is concerned, it is plausible to suggest that when people who are making progress find that their vices now engage more respectable emotions, those vices are gradually being eliminated. When Phrynis strung two extra strings on the lyre, in addition to the usual seven, the ephors asked him whether he was prepared to let them cut off the top two *or* the bottom two; but the first point to make about ourselves is that what is required is, as it were, that the top ones *and* the bottom ones are cut out, if we are going to settle on an intermediate, moderate position; and the second point is that progress begins with the lessening of our emotions' extremity and intensity, 'lusting after which,' as Sophocles says, 'makes one overwrought'.

Now, we have said that translating decisions into actions and not allowing words to be just words without turning them into deeds is particularly typical of progress. What is significant in this context is modelling our behaviour on what we commend and being keen to do what we express admiration for, while being unwilling even to connive at what we find fault with. For example, although it was not surprising that Miltiades' courage and bravery were universally applauded in Athens, nevertheless, when Themistocles said that Miltiades' trophy stopped him sleeping and allowed him no rest, it was immediately obvious that he was doing more than just expressing approbation and admiration: he was also moved to emulate and imitate Miltiades. So we must regard our progress as minimal as long as our admiration of success lies fallow and remains inadequate in itself to spur us towards imitation.

The point is that physical love is not a force for change unless it is accompanied by the desire to emulate; and commendation of virtue is also tepid and ineffective unless it nudges us and goads us to stop being envious and instead to want – with a desire that demands satisfaction – to emulate good behaviour. Alcibiades stressed the importance of the heart being moved by a philosopher's words and of tears being shed, but that is not all that is important: anyone who is making genuine progress compares his own conduct with the deeds and actions of a man who is an exemplar of goodness, and is simultaneously aggravated by the awareness of his defects, happy because of his hopes and aspirations, and full of a restless compulsion. Consequently, he is liable to 'run like an unweaned foal close to a horse' (to use a line from Semonides), because he longs to be virtually grafted on to the good man. In fact, this experience is typical of genuine progress – dearly to love the character of those whose conduct we desire to imitate, and always to accompany our wanting to be like them with goodwill which awards them respect and honour. On the other hand, anyone feeling competitively envious of his betters must realize that it is jealousy of a certain reputation or ability that is provoking him, and that he is not respecting or admiring virtue.

So when our love for good men starts to be such that we not only, as Plato says, count as blessed both the responsible man himself and anyone who listens 'to the words emitted by a responsible mouth', but we also admire and cherish his posture, walk, look and smile, and long to attach and glue ourselves to him, so to speak, then we can legitimately consider ourselves to be making genuine progress. This is even more legitimate if we do not admire only the successful aspects of men of virtue, but behave like lovers who are not put off if those they find attractive have a speech defect or a pallid complexion: despite the tears and misery brought on by her grief and misfortune, Pantheia still thrilled Araspes, and in the same way we should not be repelled by Aristides' exile, Anaxagoras' imprisonment, Socrates' poverty or Phocion's condemnation, but because we regard virtue as desirable even under these circumstances, we should draw near to it, quoting Euripides' line whenever the occasion demands – 'It's incredible how high-minded people find nothing bad!' You see, someone who is inspired enough to admire and want to imitate even apparently awful things, rather than be put off by them, can certainly never be deterred from good things ever again. It has already become such a person's practice, when he is embarking on some course of action, or taking up office, or taking a risk, to picture truly good men of the past and to wonder, 'What would Plato have done in this situation? What would Epaminondas have said? How would Lycurgus or Agesilaus have come across?' He uses each of them as a kind of mirror, before which he puts himself in order, or adjusts his stance, or refrains from some relatively petty saying of his, or resists an emotion. Some people learn the names of the Dactyls of Mount Ida and steadily recite each one, as a spell to ward off fear; but if thoughts and memories of good men readily occur to people who are making progress and make them think again, then they keep them true and safe, whatever emotions and difficulties beset them. It follows that this is another mark by which you can tell someone who is morally improving.

Moreover, to have stopped getting all flustered, blushing and hiding or rearranging some idiosyncrasy when a person who is famous for his self-control un-expectedly appears, but instead to go up to such people confidently, can corroborate one's awareness. Alexander apparently once saw a messenger running towards him with his right hand extended and looking very pleased. 'What news, my friend?' said Alexander. 'Has Homer come back to life?' For he thought that the one thing his exploits lacked was a voice that would give him undying fame. But the love which fills the character of a young man who is improving is, above all else, love of showing off before truly good people and of displaying his home, board, wife, children, occupation and spoken and written compositions; and consequently it is a source of pain for him to remember that his father or his tutor is dead and cannot see him in his present condition, and the one thing in particular he would pray to the gods for would be that they might come back to life and so witness his lifestyle and conduct. On the other hand, people who have taken no responsibility for themselves and who have been spoiled are quite the opposite: they cannot even dream about their relatives calmly and without anxiety.

There is another mark, no minor one, for you to add, please, to the ones we have already discussed. It is to have stopped regarding any of one's faults as trivial, and instead to take thorough care about and to pay attention to all of them. People who do not expect to become affluent have no qualms about spending small amounts, because they think that adding to the small amount they already have will not produce a large amount, whereas anticipation joins with savings to increase love of affluence the closer it gets to its goal. It is the same with conduct which pertains to virtue: if someone scarcely gives in to 'What's the point?' and 'That's it for now – better next time', but applies himself on every occasion, and gets fed up and irritated if vice ever worms its way, with its excuses, into even the slightest of his faults, then he is obviously in the process of acquiring for himself a certain purity and wants to avoid being defiled in any way whatsoever. On the other hand, thinking that nothing is, or can be, especially discreditable makes people nonchalant and careless about the little things. In fact, when a wall of some kind or other is being built, it does not make any difference if the odd piece of wood or ordinary stone is used as infrastructure, or if a stele that has fallen off a tomb is put in the footings, which is analogous to the conduct of degenerates who jumble together into a single heap any old business and be-haviour. But people who are progressing, and who have already 'fashioned a fine foundation' for their life (as if it were a home for gods and kings), do not admit things chosen at random, but use reason as a straight-edge by which to apply and fit every single part together. And this, in my opinion, is what Polyclitus was referring to when he said that those whose clay is at the stage when fingertips are required have the hardest task.

On the avoidance of anger

SULLA: Fundanus, I think the painters' practice of periodically examining their paintings before adding the finishing touches is commendable. Continuous familiarity hides the ways in which something might vary slightly from what is required; so by interrupting their viewing, they use repeated discrimination to keep the viewing fresh and more likely to catch minor variations. But it is impossible for a person to apply himself to himself only periodically, by separating himself and interrupting the continuity of his self-awareness – and this is the main reason why everyone is a poorer judge of himself than of others. Therefore, a second-best course is for him periodically to inspect his friends and to make himself available to them for the same purpose, which is not to see if he has suddenly grown old or if his body is in a better or worse condition, but for them to examine his habits and character, to see if over a period of time any good features have been added or bad ones subtracted.

Anyway, I've come back to Rome after over a year away, and I've been with you for over four months now. I don't find it particularly surprising that the good points you were already innately endowed with have developed and increased so much; but when I see how much more amenable and submissive to reason that strong, fiery temper of yours has become, I am inclined to comment on your impetuosity by quoting the line, 'It is amazing how much more gentle he is.'

Nevertheless, this gentleness has not made you in-effective or languid, but it has replaced your notorious sudden changes of mood with a smooth surface and an effective, productive depth – like a cultivated field. It is also clear, therefore, that your temper is not waning because advancing age has made it start to decline, or because of any other automatic factor, but because it is being treated by good rational advice. But I must confess that when our mutual friend Eros told me this about you, I suspected that his warmth towards you was making him attribute to you qualities which truly good people ought to have, even though you didn't have them – and I thought this despite the fact that, as you know, he is the last person to renounce an opinion just in order to please anyone. But I now see that he is not guilty of perjury. Since we have nothing else to do while we're travelling, I wonder if you would explain how you made your temper so tame, moderate, and amenable and obedient to reason – what regimen you followed, so to speak.

FUNDANUS: You're too kind, Sulla. Are you sure that *your* warm friendship towards me is not blinding you to some aspects of my character? I mean, even Eros himself often fails to restrain his temper and 'keep it steadily compliant' (as Homer puts it); it is righteous indignation that makes it boil over. So it is possible that I seem amenable compared to him on these occasions, just as high notes can take the place of low notes, relative to other high notes, when one scale changes into another.

SULLA: Neither of these are realistic possibilities, Fundanus. Please, as a favour to me, do what I asked.

FUNDANUS: All right. Musonius came up with some excellent suggestions, Sulla, and one of them, as I recall, was that a life of constant therapy guarantees immunity. The point is that when reason is the therapeutic agent, it should not – in my opinion – be flushed out of the system along with the illness, as hellebore is, but should remain in the mind and contain and watch over our decisions. In its effects, the analogy for reason is not medicine, but nourishing food, since anyone who becomes accustomed to it gains energy and well-being from it, whereas when emotions are at a peak of fermentation, advice and reproof struggle long and hard for slight gains, and exactly resemble smelling-salts, which arouse people who have a fit and fall unconscious, but don't get rid of the actual ailment.

Still, even at the time of their peak, all the other emotions do in a sense fall back and make way when reason with its reinforcements enters the mind from outside; but anger does not act in quite the way Melanthius says – 'It displaces intelligence and then commits criminal acts'; in fact, it does so after having replaced intelligence altogether, and shut it out of the house. And then the situation is similar to when people burn to death in their houses, in the sense that anger makes the inside full of chaos, smoke and noise, with the result that the mind is incapable of seeing or hearing anything beneficial. This is why it is easier for an abandoned ship to take on a helmsman from outside in the middle of a storm and in the open sea, than it is for someone who is being tossed in the sea of fury and anger to accept reason from an external source, unless he has made his own rationality ready. People who anticipate a siege and expect no help from outside accumulate and amass all the useful things they can; similarly, it is particularly important for people to gather from far and wide everything philosophy has to offer that will help combat anger, and to store it up in the mind – because the time when the need is crucial is also when they will not readily find it possible to introduce such assistance. I mean, the din stops the mind even hearing anything external, unless the mind has reason of its own, like an internal ship's boatswain who smartly picks up and understands every instruction; otherwise, even if the mind does hear anything, it despises quiet, gentle words and bridles at any which are more defiant. The point is that since a temper is arrogant, wilful and hard for an external agent to dislodge, it is like a secure tyranny which can be brought down only by an internal, inbred agent.

If anger becomes constant and resentment frequent, the mind acquires the negative condition known as irascibility, which results in prickliness, bitterness and a sour temper – that is, when the emotions become raw, easily distressed and hypercritical: think of a piece of iron which is already weak and thin being further filed. On the other hand, if rational discrimination immediately defies and bears down on any outburst of anger, it not only remedies the current situation, but also gives the mind energy and detachment for the future.

In my own case, at any rate, what happened is that once I had defied anger two or three times, I experienced what the Thebans did: once they had repulsed the apparently invincible Spartans for the first time, they were never subsequently defeated by them in battle. I mean, I gained the firm conviction that rationality can win. I saw that Aristotle's claim that anger ends when cold water is sprinkled on it is not the whole story: it is also quenched when faced with fear. Moreover, of course, the onset of happiness frequently causes the instantaneous 'melting', to use Homer's term, and dispersal of anger. The net result was that I became convinced that, provided the will is there, this emotion is not entirely irredeemable. You see, anger might well be aroused by something slight and meagre: often even a joke, a light-hearted remark, a laugh, a nod of assent, and so on and so forth, provoke anger. For example, when Helen addressed her niece as 'Electra, long-time spinster', she incited her remark, 'You have taken your time to see sense; in the past you left your home in disgrace.' And Callisthenes irritated Alexander by saying, when the large bowl was being passed around, 'I don't want to drink Alexander and then need Asclepius.'

Therefore, just as it is easy to control a flame which is starting to catch in hare's fur or on a wick or in a pile of rubbish (whereas if it catches in a solid object with depth, it quickly destroys and devastates 'with lively zest the lofty work of builders', as Aeschylus puts it), so anyone who pays attention to the early stages of anger and is aware of it gradually starting to smoulder and ignite as a result of some remark or rubbishy sarcasm doesn't need to exert himself a great deal, but often puts an end to it simply by keeping quiet and ignoring the remark. Anyone who doesn't fuel a fire puts it out, and anyone who doesn't feed anger in the early stages and doesn't get into a huff is being prudent and is eliminating anger.

I was accordingly not happy with Hieronymus, despite his useful comments and advice elsewhere, when he claims that because of its speed, anger is not perceptible when it is arising, but only when it has arisen and already exists. I mean, all the emotions go through the phase of gaining mass and movement, but in none of them is this arising and growth so obvious. So Homer's teaching on this is skilful: when he says, 'So he spoke; and dark clouds of anguish overshadowed Achilles', he is portraying Achilles as feeling sudden pain, when word reached him, with no lapse of time in between; but he portrays his anger at Agamemnon as slowly building up, and as gradually being ignited while a great number of words were being spoken. But if any of the people involved had withdrawn their words at the beginning and had resisted speaking them, their quarrel would not have escalated to such a degree and got so big. That is why whenever Socrates realized that he was getting too nasty to one of his friends, then because he was being driven 'as it were before a storm on the crest of an ocean wave', he used to lower his voice, smile and stop looking stern – and so keep himself upright and in control by counterbalancing the emotion and by moving instead in the opposite direction.

You see, my friend, there is a first-rate way to bring down our tyrant-like temper, which is not to listen or obey when it is ordering us to raise our voices, look fierce and beat our breasts, but to keep quiet and, as if the emotion were a disease, not aggravate it by thrashing and yelling. It may be that partying, singing and decorating doors – typical lovers' behaviour – do somehow afford an alleviation which is not unpleasing or inelegant ('I came, but did not call your name: I kissed your door. If this is a crime, I am a criminal'); and it may be that mourners eliminate a lot of their grief as well as their tears in the release of crying and weeping; but anger is made considerably more intense by the behaviour and speech of people in an angry state.

It is best, therefore, to keep calm, or alternatively to run away and hide and find refuge in silence, as though we realized that we were about to have a fit, and wanted to avoid falling, or rather falling on someone – and it is friends above all whom we most often fall on. We do not feel love or jealousy or fear for everyone, but anger leaves nothing alone, nothing in peace: we get angry at enemies and friends, at children and parents, and even at gods and animals and inanimate objects. For example, there is Thamyris, 'breaking the gilded frame, breaking the structure of the strung lyre'; and Pandarus swearing harm against himself, if he failed to burn his bow 'after shattering it with his bare hands'. And Xerxes even tried to brand and flog the sea, and sent a letter addressed to the mountain: 'Great Athos high as heaven, don't make huge, intractable rocks interfere with my actions, or else I will tear you to pieces and hurl you into the sea.' Anger can often be terrifying – but often ridiculous: that is why it is the most hated and despised of the emotions; and it is useful to be aware of both of these aspects.

In my case, at any rate – I don't know whether or not this is the correct way to go about it – I started my treatment as follows: just as the Spartans tried to understand drunkenness by watching their helots, I tried to understand anger by watching others. Hippocrates says that the severity of an illness is proportionate to the degree to which the patient's features become abnormal, and the first thing I noticed was a similar proportion between the degree of distraction by anger and the degree to which appearance, complexion, gait and voice change. This impressed upon me a kind of image of the emotion, and I was very upset to think that I might ever look so terrifying and unhinged to my friends, wife and daughters – not only fierce and unrecognizable in appearance, but also speaking in as rough and harsh a tone as I encountered in others of my acquaintance, when anger made them incapable of preserving their usual nature, appearance, pleasant conversation and persuasiveness and courtesy in company.

The orator Gaius Gracchus had a brusque personality and used to speak rather too passionately, so he had one of those little pipes made for himself which musicians use to guide their voices gradually note by note in either direction. His slave used to hold this and stand behind him while he was speaking, and sound a moderate, gentle keynote which enabled Gracchus to revoke his stridency and get rid of the harshness and anger of his tone. Just as the cowherd's 'wax-joined reed pipes in clear tones a sleep-inducing tune', so Gracchus' slave mollified and allayed the orator's anger.

If *I* had an ingenious attendant who was attuned to

me, however, I would not be displeased if he employed
a mirror during my outbursts of anger – as is occasionally
done, though for no useful purpose, for people who have
just bathed – since to see oneself in an unnatural state,
all discomposed, plays a not unimportant part in dis-
crediting the emotion. Indeed, there is an amusing story
that once when Athena was playing the pipes, a satyr
told her off by saying, 'This expression doesn't suit
you. Put down your pipes, take up your weapons and
compose your cheeks.' She paid no attention, however,
but when she saw in a river how her face looked, she
got upset and threw away the pipes.

At least art is tasteful, and this distracts one's attention from the ugliness. (Marsyas apparently used a kind
of halter and a mouthpiece to channel the force of his
breath, and to rectify and conceal the irregularity of his
features – 'gleaming gold joined the hair of one temple
to the other and thongs, bound behind, he attached to
his hard-working mouth'.) Anger, on the other hand, not
only disfigures the features by inflating and distending
them, but also makes one's voice even more ugly and
unpleasant, and 'moves the unmoved strings of the
heart'. I mean, when the sea has been whipped up by
winds and disgorges kelp and seaweed, people say that
it is being purified; but the undisciplined, harsh and snide
remarks which anger casts ashore from a mind in turmoil
pollute primarily the speakers, and contaminate them
with the opprobrium of having always had these remarks
inside them, bursting to get out, and of being exposed
by their anger. That is why, as Plato says, they pay the
heaviest of penalties for the lightest of things – a word

– since they give the impression of being antisocial, slanderous and malicious.

So when I observe and notice all this, I end up committing to memory and reminding myself pretty constantly of the fact that although when feverish it is good to have a soft, smooth tongue, it is even better when angry. I mean, if the tongue of someone with a fever is unnatural, it is a bad sign, but it does not cause any further problems; but if the tongue of someone in a temper has become rough and offensive and inclined towards abnormal language, then it manifests an insolence which causes an incurable breakdown of relationships and which betrays festering unsociability. Anger is worse than undiluted wine at producing undisciplined and disagreeable results: wine's results are blended with laughter, jokes and singing, while anger's results are blended with bitter gall; and anyone who is silent while drinking is irritating and annoying to his companions, whereas there is nothing more dignified than silence while angry, as Sappho recommends: 'When anger takes over your heart, guard your babbling tongue.'

However, constant attention to people who have been trapped by anger affords more than these reflections: it allows one to understand the nature of anger in other respects too, to see that it is not magnificent or manly, and that it has neither dignity nor grandeur. Nevertheless, most people mistake its turmoil for effectiveness, its menace for courage, its inflexibility for strength; and some people even call its callousness prowess, its stubbornness energy and its asperity righteous indignation. But this is wrong, because the actions, behaviour and conduct it prompts betray its pettiness and weakness. It is not just that angry people viciously assault little children, treat women harshly and think they should punish dogs, horses and mules (as Ctesiphon the pancratiast felt obliged to return his mule's kick); it is also that the narrow intolerance of tyrants is obvious in their cruelty, and their state is betrayed by their behaviour, so that their bloodthirstiness resembles the bite of a snake which, when enraged and in agony, directs its extreme inflammation at anyone who has hurt it. When flesh is hit hard, a swelling occurs; likewise, the most infirm minds are most liable to pain, and consequently their anger is greater because their weakness is greater.

This is also why women are more irascible than men, and sick, old or unlucky people are more irascible than healthy, middle-aged or successful people. An avaricious person is very likely to get angry with his business manager, a glutton with his cook, a jealous man with his wife, a vain person when something bad has been said about him; but the worst of all are, as Pindar says, 'political men who court ambition too much: they stir up open grief'. So it is from mental pain and suffering that anger arises, thanks above all to weakness; and whoever said that anger is, as it were, the mind's sinews was wrong: it is the straining and spraining of a mind being unduly dislocated in the course of its defensive impulses.

Anyway, observing these despicable cases was not pleasant, but simply necessary. But because I regard people who cope with fits of anger in a calm and composed manner as outstanding both to hear about and to witness, my starting-point is to despise those who say, 'You wronged a man: should a man put up with this?', and 'Tread him underfoot, tread on his neck, force him to the ground!', and so on: these are provocative things to say, and some use them improperly to transpose anger from the women's quarters to the men's. I think that manly courage is compatible with morality in all other respects, but incompatible only where gentleness is concerned, because gentleness is more self-contained. It is possible for worse men to overcome better men, but to set up in one's mind a trophy of victory over anger (which Heraclitus claims makes 'a difficult opponent, since it purchases whatever it wants at the expense of the mind') is a sign of great, overwhelming strength – a strength based on the faculties of rational judgement, which are the real sinews and muscles in the fight against the emotions.

That is why I constantly try to get hold of and read this kind of case, and not only when they are provided by philosophers (whom intelligent people regard as not being liable to gall), but even more when they are provided by kings and tyrants. For example, there is Antigonus' behaviour towards some of his soldiers who were cursing him near his tent, and didn't know he could hear them: 'Oh dear,' he said, poking his staff out of the tent and on to the ground, 'can't you go somewhere further away to criticize me?'

Arcadion the Achaean was always criticizing Philip and recommending escaping 'to a place whose inhabitants are ignorant of Philip'. Then he happened to turn up in Macedonia, and Philip's friends thought that he should punish him and not let him get away with it. Philip dealt with him kindly, however, and sent him presents and gifts; later he told his people to find out what report Arcadion had given to the Greeks. They all vouched for the fact that he had become an outstanding advocate of Philip, and Philip remarked, 'So I am a better doctor than you!' And once in Olympia some slander was being spread about him, and some people suggested that the Greeks ought to be made to suffer, since they were criticizing him despite his good treatment of them. 'What will they do, then,' he asked, 'if I treat them badly?'

Also fine was Pisistratus' behaviour towards Thrasybulus, Porsenna's towards Mucius and Magas' towards Philemon. Philemon made fun of Magas in one of his comedies, publicly in the theatre, with the lines: 'Here's a letter from the king for you to read, Magas . . . Poor Magas, what a pity you can't read!' Later, Philemon was forced into Paraetonium by a storm, and fell into Magas' hands. Magas told a soldier to unsheathe a sword and simply touch Philemon on the neck with it, and then politely leave; and he sent him dice and a ball, as if he were a witless child, and then let him go.

Ptolemy was once mocking a scholar for his ignorance and asked him who Peleus' father was; the scholar replied that he would tell him, if Ptolemy told him first who Lagus' father was. His remark was a mocking reference to the king's low-class birth, and everyone was offended, feeling that the remark jarred and was uncalled for. Ptolemy said, 'If a king can't take mockery, then he shouldn't mock either.'

Alexander had been more harsh than usual in the affairs involving Callisthenes and Clitus. So when Porus was taken prisoner by Alexander he entreated him to deal with him as a king should. 'Is that all?' asked Alexander. '"As a king should" covers everything,' replied Porus. That is why 'the benevolent' is an epithet of the king of the gods (though the Athenians call him 'the tempestuous', I think): punishment is the work of the Furies and demigods – it is not divine and Olympian.

When Philip had levelled Olynthus, someone remarked, 'But rebuilding an equivalent city will be beyond *his* capabilities'; likewise one might say to anger, 'You're good at demolition and destruction and ruination, but construction, preservation, mercy and patience require gentleness, forgiveness and moderation of passion: they require Camillus, Metellus, Aristides and Socrates, whereas plaguing and biting are what ants and mice do.'

Moreover, when I also consider vindictiveness, I find that anger's version of it is ineffective, by and large: it exhausts itself in lip-chewing, tooth-grinding, empty assaults and curses consisting of mindless threats, and the result is as ridiculous as when children in a race fall down before they reach the goal for which they are striving, because they are not in control of themselves. It follows that the Rhodian put it nicely when he said to the Roman general's servant, who was yelling and coming on strong, 'I'm not bothered by your words, but by his silence.' And once Sophocles has Neoptolemus and Eurypylus equipped with weapons, he says, 'Without making boasts, without hurling insults, the two of them smashed into the massed bronze weaponry.'

The point is that although some savages treat their weapons with poison, courage has no need of bitter gall, since it is imbued with reason, whereas anger and rage are brittle and unsound. At any rate, the Spartans play pipes to quell anger in their men while they are fighting, and before a battle they sacrifice to the Muses to ensure the stable presence of reason; and if they rout the enemy, they do not set off in pursuit, but revoke their passion, which is like those handy-sized knives in that it is retractable and manageable. Anger, however, has caused many, many people to die before exacting their revenge: Cyrus and Pelopidas of Thebes are just two examples. Agathocles, on the other hand, good-temperedly put up with insults being hurled at him by the inhabitants of a city he was besieging, and when one of them asked, 'Potter, where will you get the money to pay your mercenaries?', he replied with a laugh, 'Here, if I raze your city!' Once some people mocked Antigonus for his deformity from their city walls, and he said to them, 'But I thought I was good-looking!' But when he had taken the city, he sold the mockers into slavery, and swore that he would keep in touch with their masters, to see if they ever insulted him again.

I also notice that anger makes lawyers and orators commit great mistakes; and Aristotle records that the friends of Satyrus of Samos blocked his ears with wax when he was in court, in case he messed things up by getting angry at being abused by his opponents. As for ourselves, don't we often bungle the punishment of a slave who is misbehaving, because they get frightened at our threats and at what we are saying, and run away?

Nurses say to children, 'Stop crying and you can have it', and we could usefully address anger in the same way: 'Simmer down, shut up, slow down, and you will improve the chances and the probability of getting what you want.' I mean, if a father sees his child trying to cut or carve something with a knife, he takes the knife himself and does it; and if the rational mind takes over from anger the job of retribution, then the person who deserves it receives the punishment, and the rational mind remains safe and sound and valuable, instead of being punished itself, which is what often happens thanks to anger.

All the emotions need schooling, to tame (so to speak) and discipline by training the part of oneself that is irrational and recalcitrant; but one's servants provide a better training ground for anger than for any other emotion. The point is that our dealings with servants contain no element of envy, fear or rivalry, and constantly getting angry with them causes a lot of conflict and error and, because we have power over them, our anger puts us on a slippery downward slope, as it were, with no one to stand in our way and restrain us. I mean, absolute control cannot fail to be liable to error when emotion is involved: the only solution is to use considerable restraint to restrict your power and to resist the frequent complaints of wife and friends, as they accuse you of being weak and feeble.

I myself used to get very needled at my servants because of these accusations, and used to believe that by not punishing them I was spoiling them. But eventually I realized, first, that it is better to make them worse by patiently tolerating their badness than to concentrate on correcting others while allowing harshness and anger to corrupt oneself. And second, I saw plenty of cases where, precisely because they were not being punished, they were ashamed of being bad, let forbearance rather than retaliation initiate change in them and, I assure you, more enthusiastically served those who quietly sanctioned their actions than those who used flogging and branding: all this convinced me that reason is more authoritative than passion. The poet got it wrong when he said, 'Where there is fear, respect follows too.' It is actually the other way round: respect engenders in people the kind of fear which entails self-restraint, while non-stop, relentless flogging does not instil remorse for past misdeeds, but rather the intention to get away with it in the future.

In the third place, I constantly remind myself and bear in mind that when we were learning archery, we were not told not to shoot, but not to miss; likewise, learning how to punish in a well-timed, moderate, beneficial and appropriate way will not stop one punishing altogether. So I try to quell my anger above all by not denying the defendants the right to justify themselves, but by listening to what they have to say. This helps because time checks emotion and gives it space to dissolve, and also because rationality finds what method of punishment is appropriate, and how much is fitting. Moreover, the person who gets his just deserts has no excuse left for resisting correction, given that he is being punished not in anger, but because he has been convicted; and the most shameful factor is excluded, which is when the servant has a more just case than the master.

After Alexander's death, Phocion tried to stop the Athenians revolting too soon, or too readily trusting the news, by saying, 'If he is dead today, citizens of Athens, then he will be dead tomorrow and the day after tomorrow.' In the same way, in my opinion, anyone being driven headlong towards retaliation by anger ought to whisper to himself, 'If he is guilty today, then he will be guilty tomorrow and the day after tomorrow; and no harm will be done if he gets his just deserts later rather than sooner, but if he goes through it quickly, there will always – it has often happened in the past – be uncertainty as to his guilt.' I mean, which of us is horrible enough to flog and punish a slave for having five or ten days ago burned a savoury or knocked over a table or been rather slow to obey an order? But these are the things which make us upset and harsh and pitiless when they have just occurred and when they are still in the recent past. Solid objects seem bigger when it is misty, and the same happens to things when one is angry.

Our first reaction, therefore, should be to remember facts like this; and if in the clear, steady light of reason the deed still seems bad, when there is no doubt that we are free of the emotion, then we should attend to it: we should not at this later date neglect or abandon the punishment, as we do food when we have lost our appetite. Nothing is so conducive to doling out punishment when anger is upon us as having failed to punish, having let the issue drop, when anger had left us: the experience is identical to that of lazy rowers, who lie at anchor when the weather is calm and then run the risks of a voyage when the wind is up. We too accuse rationality of being weak and feeble when it comes to punishment, and so rush on recklessly before the wind of anger when it comes.

The point is that it is proper for someone who is hungry to engage in eating, but it is proper for someone who is neither hungry nor thirsty for it to engage in retribution. He should not need anger in order to punish, as he might need a savoury, but it is essential that he waits until he has greatly distanced himself from the appetite for punishment and introduced rationality instead. Aristotle records that in his time servants were flogged in Tyrrhenia to the accompaniment of pipes; but we should not follow suit and, for the sake of personal pleasure, be driven by a desire for satisfaction, as it were, to gorge ourselves with retaliation – to enjoy punishing (which is to behave like an animal), and then regret it later (which is to behave like a woman). Rather, we should wait until there is no trace of either pleasure or distress, and rationality is present, and then take reprisal without being motivated at all by anger.

Anyway, as may be obvious, this is not a cure for anger, but a means of postponing and protecting oneself against making mistakes while angry (despite the fact that, as Hieronymus says, although a swollen spleen is a symptom of fever, reducing the swelling alleviates the fever). But when I was trying to see how anger actually starts, I noticed that although different factors trigger its onset in different people, there is almost always present a belief that they are being slighted and ignored. It follows that we should help people who are trying to evade anger by putting the greatest possible distance between any given action and contempt or arrogance, by attributing the action instead to ignorance or necessity or emotion or accident. As Sophocles says, 'My lord, unfortunate people find that even their innate intelligence has no stability, but deserts them.' And Agamemnon attributes his theft of Briseis to his being possessed, but still says, 'I want to make amends and give you vast gifts of recompense.'

The point of this quote is that no one can make an appeal to someone if he despises him; and by being demonstrably humble, the offender gets rid of any impression of contempt. But anyone who is angry should not just wait for this to happen, but should of his own accord cling to what Diogenes said: 'Those people are laughing at you, Diogenes,' someone said; 'But I don't feel laughed at,' he replied. So anyone who is angry should not think that he is being despised, but should rather despise the other person, on the grounds that his offence was caused by weakness, impetuosity, laziness, meanness, old age or youth.

However, our dealings with servants and friends must be completely free of this impression, since contempt for us as powerless or as ineffective plays no part in their attitude towards us: our servants regard us as good, on the assumption that we are fair to them, and our friends regard us as their friends, on the assumption that we are affectionate towards them. In fact, however, it is not only wife, servants and friends that we behave harshly towards because we think we are despised by them, but the same idea often brings us into angry conflict with innkeepers, sailors and drunken muleteers, and makes us get cross with dogs for barking at us and donkeys for bumping into us. We are just like the man who wanted to hit a donkey driver, and then when he shouted, 'I'm an Athenian citizen', he said to the donkey, 'Well, *you* aren't', and began hitting it and raining blows on it.

Now, those continuous, constant feelings of anger which gradually gather in the mind like a swarm of bees or wasps are engendered in us above all by self-regard and discontent, coupled with a luxurious and enervating way of life. It follows that there is no more important means of promoting kind behaviour towards one's servants, wife and friends than being easy to please and having a simple lifestyle, as a result of the ability to adapt oneself to immediate circumstances and not to need a lot of extras. On the other hand, 'anyone whose discontent makes him critical, if his food is over-baked or over-boiled, or under- or over- or medium-seasoned', and who can't have a drink without ice, or eat shop-bought bread, or take a morsel of food served on plain or earthenware dishes, or sleep on a mattress unless it billows like the sea in a deep swell, and who flogs and beats his table servants, forcing them to hurry, making them rush about, create a hubbub and work up a sweat as if they were bringing poultices for boils – anyone like this is enslaved to a feeble, nit-picking, complaining way of life, and fails to realize that he is creating for his temper the kind of raw and oozing condition which a chronic cough or constantly bumping into things causes.

So we must train the body, by means of frugality, to be self-sufficient and hence easily pleased, because people who want little are seldom disappointed.

Food should be our starting-point: it is no great hardship quietly to make do with what is to hand, and not worry and fuss about a considerable proportion of our food, which imposes upon ourselves and our companions the most disagreeable flavouring of all – anger. It is impossible to conceive of a less pleasant meal than when servants are beaten and wife is cursed because something is burned or smoky or has insufficient salt, or because the bread is too cold. Arcesilaus once had some visitors staying and he invited friends over to dinner, but when the meal was served, there was no bread, because the servants had forgotten to buy any – which would make anyone scream loud enough to crack the walls! But Arcesilaus smiled and said, 'It's a good thing that intellectuals like a drinks party!'

Socrates once brought Euthydemus home from the wrestling-school, and Xanthippe laid into them angrily, hurled insults at them and eventually overturned the table. Euthydemus was very upset, and got up to go, but Socrates said, 'When we were at your house the other day, a hen flew in and did exactly the same, but we didn't get cross, did we?'

We should welcome friends gladly, with smiles and affection – without scowling and without instilling fear and trepidation in our servants. And we should also condition ourselves to be happy to use any utensils, and not to have preferences: some people (including Marius, we hear), having once chosen one particular goblet or cup, refuse to drink out of any other, even when they have plenty available; others are the same way about oil-flasks and strigils, and love one set above all others; and then, when any of these special things gets broken or lost, they can hardly bear it and they resort to punishment. So anyone whose weakness is anger should get rid of rare and unusual things like cups, rings and precious stones, since their loss is more unsettling than the loss of common, everyday things. That is why, when Nero had an amazingly beautiful and lavish octagonal tent made, Seneca said, 'You are a self-convicted pauper, because this tent is irreplaceable if lost.' And in fact the tent *was* lost, as it happened, when its ship went down; but Nero remembered what Seneca had said, and did not get too upset.

Being unfussy about mundane things makes one unfussy and gentle with one's servants; and if one is gentle with one's servants, then obviously one will also be gentle with one's friends and dependants. It is noticeable that the first thing slaves try to find out about their new owner, after they have been bought, is not whether he is liable to superstition or envy, but whether he has a temper. In fact, it is generally true that where anger is present, husbands cannot tolerate their wives' impassivity, or wives their husbands' passion, or friends one another's familiarity. So when anger is present, neither marriage nor friendship is endurable; but when anger is absent, even drunkenness is no burden. Dionysus' wand provides punishment enough for anyone who gets drunk, unless anger intrudes and imbues the wine with the god of cruelty and madness, rather than of ecstasy and dance. Anticyra cures straightforward insanity, but the combination of madness and anger is the stuff of tragedy and myth.

We should eliminate anger from our lighter moments, because it imposes enmity on affability; from our discussions, because it turns love of debating into love of disputing; from our decision-making, because it tinges authority with arrogance; when we are teaching, because it instils lack of confidence and a distaste for rationality; when we are doing well, because it promotes envy; when we are doing badly, because it deters sympathy by making people fight irritably with anyone commiserating with them. Priam is an example of this, with his 'Go away, you vile wretches! Haven't you got problems of your own? Why have you come to bother me?'

Being easy to please, on the other hand, is either a help or an embellishment or a delight, and its gentleness overcomes anger and discontent of all kinds. Consider Euclides, for instance: when his brother ended an argument by saying, 'I'll get my own back on you, if it's the last thing I do', Euclides replied, 'I'll win you over, if it's the last thing *I* do', and immediately made him alter course and change his mind. And Polemon was once being cursed by a man who was fond of precious stones and obsessed with costly rings; Polemon did not respond at all, but began to study one of the man's rings closely. So the man felt pleased and said, 'You'll get a far better impression of it, Polemon, if you examine it in sunlight rather than here.'

Once Aristippus was angry with Aeschines, and someone asked, 'What's happened to Aeschines', and your friendship, Aristippus?' He replied, 'It's sleeping, but I'll wake it up.' He went to Aeschines and said, 'Do you think there's absolutely no chance for me, no hope at all? Is that why you don't tell me off?' And Aeschines' response was: 'Given that you're inherently better than me in all respects, it's not at all surprising that you were the first to see what to do.'

It has been said that 'A new-born child, stroking a bristle-maned boar with his young hand, may – and so may a woman – bring him down more easily than any wrestler.' We, however, domesticate and tame wild creatures, and carry wolf and lion cubs around in our arms, but then under the influence of anger we reject children, friends and acquaintances; and we use our anger like a wild beast to assault our servants and fellow citizens, and misguidedly gloss over it as 'right-eous indignation'. There is no difference, in my opinion, between this and calling other mental affections and afflictions 'foresight' or 'independence' or 'respect': it cannot free us from any of them.

Now, Zeno used to say that seed is a compound, a mixture of extracts from all the faculties which make up a person's nature; and analogously, anger seems to be a kind of conglomerate of emotional seeds. It contains elements extracted from pain and pleasure and arro-gance; it has the gloating pleasure of spite, and also gets its method of grappling from spite, in the sense that the avoidance of its own suffering is not the purpose of its efforts, but it accepts harm to itself while destroying the other person; and one of its ingredients is the form of desire which is the most disagreeable of all, the longing to hurt someone else. When we approach reprobates' houses, we hear a pipe-girl playing at dawn and the sights that greet our eyes are, to quote, 'sediment of wine and shreds of garlands' and inebriated servants at the door; but the fact that the longing to hurt others is an aspect of anger explains why you will see the manifest signs of cruel and irascible people on the faces and in the identification tattoos and chains of their servants; and 'wailing is the only constant refrain to arise in the house' of an angry man – the wailing of estate-managers being flogged and serving-women having their arms twisted inside the house; and the consequence of all this is that anger is pitiful to anyone who can see that its desires and its pleasures involve pain.

Despite what has been said, anyone who is commonly susceptible to anger because of genuine righteous indignation must rid himself of the excessive, unmitigated part of his anger, along with his overconfidence in the people he comes across. This overconfidence is one of the chief causes of the aggravation of anger, which is what happens when someone assumed to be good turns out to be bad, or when a supposed friend gets cross or critical. In my own case, I'm sure you know how much I am naturally inclined towards thinking well of people and trusting them. It is like when you take a step, but there is nothing there to tread on: the more I commit myself to being friendly, the more I go wrong and get hurt by my mistakes. I might well not be able at this late stage to lessen this excessive susceptibility to and enthusiasm for friendship; but I can use Plato's words of warning to bridle my overconfidence. Plato says that his praise for the mathematician Helicon is couched the way it is because Helicon is a member of an inherently inconstant species; and he claims to be right to be wary of people brought up in his city, because since they are human and the offspring of humans, they might at any time reveal the weakness inherent in their nature.

However, Sophocles' assertion that 'Most aspects of humanity will be found on investigation to be contemptible' seems excessively harsh and restrictive. Still, the pessimistic, carping tone of this judgement does make us less liable to anger and its consequent disruptiveness; I mean, it is what is unexpected and unforeseen that throws us. We should (as Panaetius said at one point) make use of the attitude summed up in Anaxagoras' dictum: when his son died, he said, 'I knew that I had fathered a mortal.' Likewise, whenever we get irritated by someone's mistakes, we should comment, 'I knew that the slave I bought was unintelligent', or 'I knew that my friend was not flawless', or 'I knew that my wife was a woman.' And if one also keeps reiterating Plato's saying, 'Am I not like that too?', he will turn his thinking inward instead of outward, and will interrupt his complaining with caution, and will consequently not employ a great deal of righteous indignation towards others when he sees that he himself requires a lot of forbearance. But as it is, every one of us gets angry and lashes out, and sounds like Aristides and Cato: 'Stop stealing!', 'Don't tell lies!', 'Why are you slacking?' And the most despicable thing of all is that we angrily reprimand others for being angry, and we furiously punish others for mistakes made because they were infuriated: we do not behave like doctors who 'use bitter medicine to flush out bitter bile', but we aggravate and exacerbate the condition.

At the same time as bearing in mind these considerations, I also try to cut back a bit on my nosiness. I mean, knowing every single detail about everything, investigating and eliciting a slave's every occupation, a friend's every action, a son's every pastime, a wife's every whisper – this leads to many outbursts of anger, one after another every day, and these in turn add up to habitual discontent and surliness. Although Euripides is right to say that it is when things get out of hand that God 'intervenes, while leaving minor matters to chance', I still think that a sensible person ought to entrust nothing to chance, and ought to ignore nothing: he should trust and make use of his wife for some matters, his servants for others and his friends for others (just as a ruler trusts and makes use of overseers, accountants and managers), while being himself, by virtue of his rationality, in charge of the most far-reaching and important matters. For just as tiny writing irritates the eyes, so the extra strain of trivial matters chafes and unsettles one's temper, and it acquires a habit which is detrimental when more important matters are at stake.

All in all, therefore, I began to think that Empedocles' dictum 'Observe a fast from evil' is crucial and inspired; furthermore, not just because they are agreeable, but also because they are not irrelevant to the practice of philosophy, I began to commend those familiar pacts, pledged with devotion, such as to honour God with one's self-control, by keeping oneself for a year untainted by sex and alcohol; or again to refrain from lying for a prescribed period of time, by paying attention to oneself to make sure that one always tells the truth, in both unguarded and serious moments.

And then I compared my own pledge with these, and found it just as pleasing to God and just as sacred. My pledge was to begin by spending a few days doing the equivalent of going without drinking and alcohol – avoiding anger, and doing so as if I were pouring ritual libations of water and of honey, but not of wine; and then to spend a month, two months, doing this . . . In this way, by experimenting on myself, the period of time gradually got longer and I progressed towards increased tolerance, by using self-control to pay attention to myself and to keep myself composed and imperturbable – maintaining a holy silence – and to remain untainted by pernicious speech, unnatural actions and emotion. Emotion leads, for the sake of a form of pleasure which is small in quantity and disagreeable in quality, to enormous mental confusion and the most despicable remorse. And this, I think, is why (with God's assistance too) my experience tends to clarify the meaning of the well-known view that this composure, calmness and charity is nowhere near as kind and considerate and inoffensive to those who come across it as it is to those who possess it.

On contentment

FROM PLUTARCH TO PACCIUS. I hope this finds you well. Not long ago, I got your letter, in which you suggested that I write down for you something about contentment, and about those passages in *Timaeus* which need rather careful interpretation. At pretty much the same time, our friend Eros suddenly found he had to sail to Rome, since he had received a letter from the illustrious Fundanus; typically, Fundanus told him to hurry. On the one hand, I didn't have as much time as I wanted to get to grips with the topics you were asking me to address; but on the other hand, I couldn't bear the idea of Eros leaving here, going to you and being found to be completely empty-handed. So I read those bits of my notebooks, written in fact for myself, which covered the topic of contentment. I imagined that what you too wanted from this discourse was practical help, not a lecture whose aim was elegant composition; and I share your pleasure in the fact that although you have friends in positions of authority, and although you have a pre-eminent reputation as a political speaker, you have not experienced what Merops did in the tragedy: it is not the case, as it was with him, that 'the adulation of the masses has driven you mad' and into abnormal behaviour. No, you have taken to heart what you have often been told: 'gout is not alleviated by a patrician shoe, nor a whitlow by an expensive ring nor a migraine by a crown.' How on earth can assets or a reputation or power at court contribute towards having a mind that is free of distress and a life that is as calm as a millpond, unless their possession and use are pleasant, but at the same time they are never missed if they are lacking? And what else guarantees this except rationality which has become accustomed to quickly restraining – and taking care to do so – the emotional, irrational part of the mind on the many occasions when it tries to exceed its bounds, and not conniving at its flooding and racing away from what is actually there?

Xenophon recommends that we remember and acknowledge the gods particularly in times of prosperity, so that when we are in need, we can confidently petition them in the knowledge that they are predisposed to be charitable and friendly. It is no different in the case of rational arguments which help us combat the emotions: anyone with any sense should pay attention to them before emotion arises, so as to widen his defensive preparations and thereby increase the benefit he gains. You know how aggressive dogs get thoroughly agitated at any and every loud voice and are calmed down only by the one with which they are familiar; so the mind's emotions too are hard to restrain when they are overexcited, unless rational arguments are already there, ingrained and familiar, to check the agitation.

Whoever it was who said that 'Contentment is impossible for anyone who busies himself with personal or public affairs' makes contentment, in the first place, an expensive commodity if its price is inactivity. It is as though his prescription for every invalid is to say, 'You poor thing, stay perfectly still in your bed', whereas inertia is in fact no good as a treatment for a body suffering from numbness and, as psychiatry, it is equally ineffective to try to remove agitation and distress from the mind by means of laziness, weakness and betrayal of friends, household and country.

Moreover, in the second place, it is not true that anyone who is not busy is content. It would follow that women are more content than men, since they generally deal only with domestic matters; but in fact, although (in Hesiod's words) the north wind 'does not reach a young woman's tender body', nevertheless distress, disturbance and depression trickle into the women's quarters through the agency of jealousy, superstition, ambition and innumerable empty beliefs. Laertes spent twenty years by himself away from civilization, 'with an old woman to look after him, who served his food and drink', and although he shunned his country, home and kingdom, nevertheless his inactivity and ennui had distress as a constant close companion. Even absolute inactivity is likely to induce discontent in some cases: for example, 'But swift-footed Achilles, Peleus' son, descended from Zeus, stayed sitting by his sharp-prowed ships and never went to assembly, which brings men prestige, or to battle, but stayed there with his heart pining in longing for the war cry and for battle.' The depth of his feeling and his grief caused him to say to himself, 'I sit by my ships, a pointless burden to the world.'

This is why not even Epicurus thinks that a quiet life

is desirable; he says that people who want status and fame should go along with this aspect of their nature and engage in politics and public life, because they are inherently more likely to be thrown off balance and to be harmed by inactivity – by failing to fulfil their desires. But it is ridiculous for him to recommend public life, not to those with talent, but to those who are incapable of living peacefully. Contentment and discontent should be defined not by the frequency or rarity of one's actions, but by their goodness or badness: the omission of good deeds is – and this has been said before – just as annoying and disturbing as the commission of bad deeds.

There are people who think that freedom from distress resides in one way of life in particular – for instance, in farming or bachelorhood or kingship. What Menander said can act as a reminder for them: 'Phanias, I used to think that rich people, because they have no debts, don't sigh at night, or toss and turn, or moan "Poor me!"; I used to think they slept a pleasant, peaceful sleep.' He goes on to explain that, in his experience, even the rich suffer exactly as the poor do, and then says, 'Is grief related in some way to life? It consorts with a life of luxury, is inseparable from a life of fame, grows old with a life of poverty.'

Consider people who are scared of sailing or who get seasick: they imagine that the voyage will pass more easily if they exchange a skiff for a merchant ship, and then the merchant ship for a trireme; but this gets them nowhere, because they take their sickness and fears with them. This is an analogy for exchanging one way of life for another; it does not eradicate from the mind the factors which make it distressed and disturbed, which are unworldliness, lack of discrimination and not being able, or not knowing how, to make proper use of one's present circumstances. These are the storm winds that vex both rich and poor, trouble both married and single; they make men shun public life and then find a quiet life intolerable; they make men pursue promotion at court and be miserable as soon as they get it. 'Helplessness makes sick people a peevish lot': their wives irritate them, they complain about their doctors, grumble about their beds and 'for a friend to come is a nuisance, to leave is an offence', as Ion says. But when the illness has dissolved and the humours are differently blended, health comes and makes everything nice and pleasant, in the sense that someone who yesterday detested eggs and cakes and bread made from fresh wheat, today is even glad to eat coarse bread with olives or mustard seeds.

The engendering of rationality within us causes this kind of satisfaction with, and change of attitude towards, any way of life. Alexander once shed tears while listening to Anaxarchus lecture on the existence of an infinite number of worlds. His friends asked him what the matter was, and he replied, 'Don't you think tears are called for, if there are an infinite number of worlds, and I've not yet gained control of just one?' On the other hand, Crates, with his bag and threadbare cloak, spent his whole life joking and laughing as though he were on holiday. Moreover, Agamemnon was troubled by his extensive responsibilities as king – 'You will recognize Agamemnon, son of Atreus, whom Zeus has singled out for constant hard work' – but when Diogenes was up for sale, he lay on the ground and teased the auctioneer by refusing to get up when told to, but joking and saying with a laugh, 'Imagine it's a fish you're trying to sell!' Or again, Socrates went on discussing philosophy with his companions while he was in prison, but Phaethon used to weep when he had scaled the heights of heaven, if no one gave him his father's horses and chariot.

It is the shoe that bends along with the foot, not the other way around; and likewise, an implication of what we have been saying is that disposition moulds life. I mean, the notion that familiarity makes the best life pleasant for anyone who has chosen it is wrong: it is rational intelligence which makes the life one already has both the best one and the most pleasant one. It follows that we should purify our innate well of contentment and then external things will be in harmony with us too, provided we don't maltreat them, and will seem congruent and congenial. 'There's no point in getting angry with one's situation, because it is utterly indifferent; but success will accrue to anyone who treats the situations he encounters correctly.'

Plato compared life to a game of dice in which it is not just important to throw something appropriate, but also to make good use of it however the throw turns out. And where our situations are concerned, it may be true that we do not control the throw of the dice, but it is our job, if we are sensible, to accommodate ourselves to whatever fortune deals us and to allocate everything to a place where, as each situation arises, if it is congruent, we can maximize its benefit, and if it is unwelcome, we can minimize its harm. A physical illness can make people incapable of enduring either heat or cold, and those who muddle unintelligently through life are like that, in the sense that they get ecstatic at good fortune and depressed at bad fortune – which is to say that both good and bad fortune knock them off balance, or rather that they knock themselves off balance when they encounter either of them; and it is the same story when they encounter anything that one might term good. Theodorus the Atheist (as he was called) used to say that although he delivered his lectures with his right hand, the audience caught them in their left hands; and uneducated people, faced with a favourable or right-handed opportunity, often take it up awkwardly or left-handedly and make fools of themselves. Thyme, the most acrid and dry of plants, provides bees with honey; and likewise intelligent people can invariably find something congruent with and useful to themselves from the most forbidding of situations.

The chief thing, then, to practise and pursue is the attitude exemplified by the man whose stone missed his dog and hit his stepmother: 'That's not bad either!' he said. It is possible to change opportunities so that they are no longer unwelcome. Diogenes was exiled; 'That's not bad either', because he subsequently took up philosophy. Zeno of Citium had just one ship left from his merchant fleet; when he was told that this one too was lost, sunk with all its cargo, he said, 'Thank you, fortune, for helping to drive me into a threadbare cloak.'

Why can't the rest of us behave in the same way? Have you failed to capture some public position you were after? You can live in the country, minding your *own* business. Have you been spurned while courting the affection of someone in authority? You can now live a life free of risk and bother. Is your time again taken up with worldly business and worries? Well, to quote Pindar, 'the extent to which warm water relaxes a body is nothing' compared to how fame and respect, conjoined with power, make 'work pleasant and labour non-laborious'. Are you faced with misery and insults because lies or malicious tales are being spread about you? This is a following wind, blowing you towards the Muses and the Academy, as Plato was driven by the storm winds of his friendship for Dionysius.

It follows that another thing that is important for contentment is to reflect on famous men, and how they have not been affected at all by circumstances identical to one's own. Is childlessness your problem, for example? Look at the kings of Rome, none of whom had a son to whom he could bequeath his kingdom. Are you weighed down by poverty at the moment? But is there any Boeotian you would rather be than Epaminondas, any Roman rather than Fabricius? 'But my wife has been seduced!' Well, haven't you read the inscription at Delphi which goes 'Erected by Agis, lord of water and of earth'? And haven't you heard that this is the man whose wife Timaea was seduced by Alcibiades, and that in an undertone to her serving-women she used to call her child Alcibiades? Yet this did not stop Agis from being the most famous and important Greek of his day. Nor, for example, did the promiscuity of Stilpo's daughter stop him living a more carefree life than any of his philosophical contemporaries. In fact, when Metrocles told him off for his daughter's behaviour, Stilpo's response was, 'Is it my fault or hers?' Metrocles said, 'Her fault, but your misfortune.' 'What do you mean?' asked Stilpo. 'Isn't a fault a mistake?' 'Certainly,' said Metrocles. 'And isn't anyone making a mistake also suffering a setback?' continued Stilpo. Metrocles agreed. 'And isn't anyone suffering a setback also suffering a misfortune?' Stilpo concluded. This calm, philosophical argument showed the Cynic's aspersion to be empty barking.

Still, most people *are* hurt and provoked, by their enemies' flaws, as well as by those of their friends and relatives. I mean, being inclined towards insolence, anger, spite, malice, jealousy and hostility not only plagues those people who have these weaknesses, but also annoys and irritates foolish people – as, of course, do a neighbour's short temper, an acquaintance's grumpiness and a public administrator's iniquity. And I think that you too are very far from failing to get upset at these flaws; like the doctors in Sophocles who 'use bitter medicine to flush out bitter bile', you react to these affections and affictions with rage and bitterness. But this is unreasonable, because the public business which has been entrusted to you and which you conduct is managed by people whose characters are not straight-forward and good, as well-made tools should be, but are invariably jagged and warped; and you should not, therefore, consider it to be your job – or at any rate you should not consider it to be an easy job – to straighten them out. However, if you use them as a doctor uses tooth extractors and wound clamps – that is, as being made just the way they are – and if you show your-self to be as lenient and moderate as circumstances permit, then your pleasure in your own attitude will outweigh your distress at others' unsatisfying and iniqui-tous behaviour, you will regard them as doing what comes naturally to them (as dogs are when they bark) and you will stop unwittingly being infected by others' flaws, which is to let plenty of distressing factors seep into the sunken and low-lying land of this pettiness and weakness of yours.

Some philosophers find fault even with compassion, when it is felt for people who are out of luck, on the grounds that while helping people one comes across is a good thing, sharing their troubles and giving in to them is not. More importantly, they forbid us to be discon-tented or depressed even when we realize that we our-selves have flawed and defective characters; they tell us instead not to get distressed, but just to try to cure the problem, as is right and proper. You should consider, then, how utterly illogical it is for us to connive at ourselves getting cross and irritated because not every-one with whom we have dealings and who crosses our paths is fair and congenial.

No, my dear Paccius, you must make sure that we are not deceiving ourselves by denouncing and being worried about the iniquity of people we come across only in so far as it affects us, rather than in general – that is, you must make sure that we are not being motivated by selfishness, but by hatred of badness. The point is that if we are unduly discomposed by public life and if we have unwarranted impulses and aims, or alternatively unwarranted aversions and antipathies, then this makes us suspicious of people and irritated by them, because we think that they are the causes of our losses and accidents. A high degree of contentment and calmness in relating to people is an attribute of someone who has trained himself to cope with public life without fuss and bother.

Bearing this in mind, let us return to the matter of one's situation. When we have a fever, everything tastes bitter and unpleasant, but once we have seen other people taking the same food without revulsion, we stop blaming the food and drink, and start to blame ourselves and our illness. In the same way, we will stop blaming and being disgruntled at circumstances if we see other people cheerfully accepting identical situations without getting upset. So when unwelcome incidents occur, it is also good for contentment not to ignore all the gratifying and nice things we have, but to use a process of blending to make the better aspects of our lives obscure the glare of the worse ones. But what happens at the moment is that, although when our eyes are harmed by excessively brilliant things we look away and soothe them with the colours that flowers and grasses provide, we treat the mind differently: we strain it to glimpse the aspects that hurt it, and we force it to occupy itself with thoughts of the things that irritate it, by tearing it almost violently away from the better aspects. And yet the question addressed to the busybody can be transferred to this context and fit in nicely: 'You spiteful man, why are you so quick to spot someone else's weakness, but overlook your own?' So we might ask: why, my friend, do you obsessively contemplate your own weakness and constantly clarify it and revivify it, but fail to apply your mind to the good things you have? Cupping-glasses extract from flesh anything particularly bad, and likewise you are attracting to yourself the very worst of your attributes. You are making yourself no better at all than the Chian who used to sell plenty of quality wine to other people, but for his own meal used to taste wines until he found a vinegary one; and when someone asked one of his servants what he had left his master doing, the servant replied, 'Looking for bad when surrounded by good.'

As a matter of fact, most people do bypass what is good and refreshing in their lives, and make straight for the unpleasant, bad elements. Aristippus was different, however: he was good at lightening himself and raising himself up (imagine him on a pair of scales) towards the better aspects of his situation. At any rate, he once lost a fine estate, and people were insincerely saying how sorry and sympathetic they felt. He asked one of them, 'Haven't you got just one little plot of land, while I have still got three farms?' The fellow said yes, and Aristippus said, 'Why, then, am I not feeling sorry for you, rather than the other way round?' The point is that it is crazy to be upset about what one has lost and not feel happy about what one has kept; otherwise, we are behaving like little children who, when deprived of just one of their many toys, wail and scream and throw all the rest of their toys away. In the same way, if we let fortune distress us just once, then our whining and resentment deprives everything else as well of any benefit for us.

Someone might ask, 'But what can we be said to have or not to have?' Fame, property, married status, a good friend – these are the things people have. When Antipater of Tarsus was close to death, he added up the good things that had happened to him, and included even the easy voyage he had had from Cilicia to Athens. And we must not overlook even things we share with others, but take them into account, and be thankful that we have life and health and that we walk the earth; that there is no war, either foreign or civil, but that we may, if we so choose, farm the land and sail the seas without fear; that the full range of possibilities is open to us, from oratory and politics to a quiet, inactive life. When we have these shared things, we will increase our contentment with them if we imagine that we do not have them, and frequently remind ourselves how desirable health is to sick people, peace to people at war, and the acquisition of fame and friends to an obscure stranger in a city as big as yours, and also remind ourselves how distressing it is to lose these things if they have been ours in the past. If we do this, then we will not rate and value any of these things highly only once it has been lost, while discounting it altogether as long as it is in our keeping. I mean, the fact that we do not own something does not increase its value; and we should not be acquisitive as if these things were important, and be constantly trembling in fear of losing them as if they were important, but ignore them and belittle them, while we have them, as if they were worthless. Instead, while we have them, we should above all use them for our enjoyment and profit from them, so that, in the event of their loss, we can endure this too with greater equanimity. Arcesilaus used to point out that although most people think it their duty to use their minds to explore and their eyes to examine other people's poems, paintings and statues in precise and minute detail, yet they forget their own lives, which could provide plenty of areas for pleasurable reflection: they constantly look outwards and are impressed by other people's fame and fortune, just as adulterers are by other men's wives, but belittle themselves and what they already have.

Nevertheless, another thing that is important for contentment is to restrict one's inspection as much as possible to oneself and those things which are relevant to oneself, or else to consider people who are less well off than oneself. What one should avoid is lining oneself up against people who are better off, despite the fact that this is the usual practice: prisoners, for instance, envy those who have been freed, who envy people who have always been free, who envy those with citizen status, who in turn envy rich people, who envy province commanders, who envy kings, who – because they almost aspire to making thunder and lightning – envy the gods. Consequently, since they never attain things which are out of their reach, they are never thankful for the things that are relevant to them. 'Gold-laden Gyges' possessions are of no interest to me; I have never yet been gripped by envy, nor do I seek to emulate what the gods do, nor do I desire a great kingdom. I do not set my sights on such distant views.'

Someone might say, 'That's because this is a Thasian speaking.' But there are other provincials – from Chios,

Galatia or Bithynia – who are dissatisfied with having obtained a portion of status or power among their compatriots, and who weep because they do not wear patrician robes; and if they do, then because they have not yet held military command at Rome; and if they have, then because they are not consuls; and if they are, then because when the announcement was made, they did not head the list. The only possible description of this is self-mortification and self-inflicted punishment, as a result of scrabbling for reasons to be ungrateful to fortune. On the other hand, anyone whose mind sanely reflects that the sun sees countless thousands of humans – 'all we who enjoy the broad land's produce' – does not slump into depression and despondency if there are people more famous and rich than himself; there are so many human beings that his life is a thousand times more perfect than thousands of people's, so he continues on his path, celebrating his own destiny and life.

It may be impossible to choose one's opponents in the Olympic Games and so gain victory that way, but life's situations do often present one with opportunities for appreciating one's better position – for being envied rather than envying others – unless, of course, it is Briareus or Heracles one pits oneself against! So when you find yourself overawed by the apparent superiority of a man who is being carried in a sedan chair, make sure you look down and also see those who are keeping him off the ground; and when you find yourself envying Xerxes, as the Hellespontian did, on the famous occasion of Xerxes' pontoon crossing, make sure you also see the men being driven by whips to excavate Mount Athos and the men with faces mutilated when the bridge was destroyed by the waves; if you take *their* thoughts into consideration as well, you find that they are envying your life and your situation.

Socrates once heard one of his acquaintances remarking how expensive Athens was: 'A mina for Chian wine, three minae for a purple-dyed robe, five drachmae for a *kotyle* of honey.' Socrates grabbed hold of him and showed him some grain – 'An obol for half a *hekteus* – Athens is cheap'; and then some olives – 'Two bronze coins for a *choinix* – Athens is cheap'; and then some simple cloaks – 'Ten drachmae – Athens is cheap.' So when we too hear someone remarking on how trivial and terribly distressing our personal situations are, because we are not consuls or governors, we can reply, 'Our situations are not at all unprepossessing, and our lives are to be envied, because we are not beggars or porters or flatterers.'

Despite all this we habitually live, out of stupidity, with our attention on others rather than on ourselves. So since human nature contains plenty of malicious envy and spite, with the result that the degree of pleasure we feel in what is ours is less than the degree of irritation we feel at others' successes, then you must not only notice the splendid and pre-eminent features of the people you envy and admire, but you must also remove and draw aside the florid veil, so to speak, of their reputation and their façade, and get inside, where you will notice that they contain plenty of unsavoury features and plenty of unpleasantness. At any rate, something Pittacus said is instructive, since he is outstandingly famous for courage, wisdom and morality: he once had some friends round for dinner, and his wife burst in angrily and overturned the table; his friends were astounded, but he said, 'No one's life is perfect; anyone with only my troubles is very well off.'

'In public this man is an object of envy, but as soon as he opens the door of his home, he's in a pitiful state: his wife is in complete control, she bosses him about and argues all the time. He's got rather a lot of reasons to be miserable, whereas I've got none.' Plenty of these kinds of troubles accompany wealth, fame and kingship, but most people fail to notice them under the showy veneer. 'Son of Atreus, you are fortunate – your birth was favoured by fate and your destiny is to prosper': this kind of accolade is given for weaponry, horses and an extensive army, for external possessions, but from within come the contradictory emotional cries, bearing witness against this hollow fame – 'Zeus the son of Cronus has thoroughly imprisoned me in deep madness' and 'I envy you, old man, and I envy anyone whose life is at an end, if he has kept himself safe by avoiding recognition and fame.' Here is another point we should bear in mind, then, to enable us to carp less against fortune and to decrease the extent to which, by admiring our acquaintances' attributes, we belittle and denigrate our own.

Now, a major impediment to contentment is the failure to keep our desires furled or unfurled, so to speak, in a way which is commensurate with the prevailing potential. Instead, we give them too much slack through our hopes, and then when we fail, we blame fate and fortune, but not our own stupidity. We wouldn't describe as unfortunate anyone who wanted to shoot with his plough and hunt hares with his cow, nor would we say that anyone who fails to capture deer or boar with fishing-baskets or seines is being opposed by bad luck: it is stupidity and silliness which are setting him to impossible endeavours. The chief cause is in fact self-love, which makes people ambitious and competitive whatever the situation, and makes them greedily take on everything: they not only expect to be rich, erudite, strong, outgoing, pleasant and intimate with kings and leaders of nations, but they are discontented if their dogs, horses, quails and cocks are not the best at what they do.

Dionysius the Elder was not satisfied with being the most important tyrant of the time, but because his verse was worse than that of Philoxenus the poet, and he failed to do better than Plato at philosophical discussion, he got furiously angry – he imprisoned Philoxenus in the quarries, and he sent Plato to Aegina to be sold into slavery. Alexander was different: when the sprinter Crison was racing with him and gave the impression of deliberately slowing down, Alexander was very cross. And Achilles in the poem does well too: he starts off saying, 'None of the bronze-clad Achaeans is my equal', but goes on, 'in war; but there are those who are better in assembly.' On the other hand, when Megabyzus the Persian visited Apelles' studio and tried to start a conversation about art, Apelles shut him up by saying, 'As long as you kept quiet, you seemed to be someone because of your golden jewellery and purple-dyed clothes, but

now even these lads here who grind the pigment are
laughing at you for talking nonsense.'

Now, although people might think, when they hear
the Stoic description of the sage not only as wise, moral
and courageous, but also as an orator, poet and military
commander, as possessing wealth and as a king, that
they are joking, nevertheless they expect all these descrip-
tions for themselves and are annoyed if they don't get
them. Yet even different gods have different functions –
one being called the god of battle, another the god of
prophecy, another the god of profit; and Aphrodite is
ordained by Zeus to preside over marriage and sex,
precisely because her domain does not include military
matters.

The point is that some pursuits inherently do not go
together, but rather tend in opposite directions. For
instance, rhetorical training and the acquisition of intel-
lectual disciplines need freedom and no pressure, but
political power and intimacy with kings do not accrue
without one being busy and using up one's time. Moreover, 'drinking wine and overeating meat may make the
body strong and robust, but they weaken the mind'; and
whereas constant concern and care for money increase
affluence, yet disdain and scorn for money constitute an
important resource for philosophy. So not everything is
for everyone: one should follow the Delphic inscription
and know oneself, and then engage in the single activity
for which one is naturally suited; and one should avoid
forcibly and unnaturally compelling oneself to envy
alternative ways of life – and different ones at different
times. 'A horse is harnessed to a cart, an ox to a plough;

a dolphin darts with great rapidity by a ship; and whoever plans death for a boar must find a courageous dog.'

Anyone, however, who is upset and distressed because he is not simultaneously a lion, 'mountain-reared, confident in his might', and a little Maltese dog protected in the lap of a widow, is crazy – but no crazier than anyone who wants to be Empedocles, Plato or Democritus, writing about the universe and the way things really are, and at the same time a Euphorion, with a rich older woman for a lover, or a Medius, hobnobbing with Alexander as one of his drinking companions, and gets irritated and distressed if he isn't an Ismenias, admired for his affluence, and an Epaminondas, admired for his goodness. I mean, runners aren't discontented because they don't win the wrestling competition: they find pride and satisfaction in their own prizes. 'You have obtained Sparta, so do it credit.' And, as Solon says, 'We will not exchange our virtue for their wealth, since the one is stable, but different people have money at different times.'

When Strato, the natural philosopher, was told that Menedemus' students far outnumbered his, he said, 'What else would you expect? There are bound to be more people who want to bathe than want to put oil on their bodies.' And Aristotle wrote to Antipater, 'The fact that Alexander rules over a lot of people does not make him the only one who can legitimately feel proud: anyone whose thinking about the gods is correct has just as much right.' The point is that people who value what they have, as in these stories, are not upset by whatever anyone else they come across has. But what happens at the moment is that although we do not expect a vine to produce figs or an olive to produce grapes, yet if we don't have the advantages of both plutocrats and scholars, military commanders and philosophers, flatterers and those who speak their minds, misers and big spenders, all at once, we bully ourselves, are dissatisfied with ourselves, and despise ourselves as living deficient and unfulfilled lives.

In addition, there are also clear reminders from nature. Different animals have been differently equipped by nature to provide for themselves: they have not all been made carnivores or seed-peckers or root-diggers. In the same way, nature has granted a wide variety of means of living to human beings – 'to shepherd, ploughman, bird-catcher and to the man whose livelihood comes from the sea'. What we should do, then, is choose what suits our specific natures, work at it and forget others' occupations; in other words, we should not show up any deficiency in Hesiod's assertion that 'Potter is jealous of potter, builder of builder.' I mean, people do not try to emulate only others with the same profession and same way of life; instead, rich men envy scholars and are in turn envied by famous people, while lawyers envy professional orators and – strange though it may seem – free men and aristocrats are utterly in awe of what they see as the happiness of comic actors in successful plays, and of dancers and servants in the royal courts. The result is that they distress and discompose themselves a great deal.

It is clear from the differences between people's experiences that everyone has within himself the resources which may lead to contentment or discontent – the jars of good and bad do not sit 'on Zeus's threshold', but lie in our minds. Foolish people overlook and ignore good things even when they are present, because their thoughts are always straining towards the future; intelligent people, on the other hand, use their memories to keep them vivid for themselves even when they are no longer present. Anything present is accessible for the minutest fraction of time and then escapes perception, and consequently foolish people think that it ceases to be relevant to us, or ceases to be ours. There is a painting of a man in Hades weaving a rope, who lets it out to a donkey at pasture, which eats up what he is weaving; in exactly the same way, most people succumb to blind, ungrateful oblivion, which consumes them and leaves no trace of any event, any moment of success, pleasant relaxation, interaction or delight.

This oblivion prevents life being a unity of past events woven with present ones: it divides yesterday from today, as if they were distinct, and likewise treats tomorrow as different from today, and it immediately consigns every occurrence to non-existence by never making use of memory. The school of thought which eliminates growth on the assumption that being is in constant flux makes each person, in theory, different from himself, and then different again; similarly, those who don't use memory to protect or recover what has gone before, but let it trickle away, day by day, make themselves in fact incomplete and empty and in suspense for the day to follow, as if the events of last year, the recent past and yesterday had no bearing on them or, in short, didn't happen to them.

So this is another thing that unsettles contentment, but not as much as the next factor we must consider. You know how when flies settle on mirrors, they skid off the smooth parts but cling on to places which are rough and scratched; this is an analogy for how people slide away from happy, congenial matters and get caught up in their memories of unpleasant things. An even better analogy might be based on the story that in Olynthus there is a place (called 'Beetle-death') which beetles fall into and are unable to get out of: they go round and round in circles until they die there. Likewise, without noticing it, people slip into recalling their bad times and are unwilling to revive or resuscitate themselves.

What we should do is treat the mind like a painting, and the events the mind recalls like the colours, and so give prominence to what is bright and vivid, and push anything gloomy into the obscurity of the background. I mean, it is impossible to eradicate and exclude the gloomy aspects altogether: 'The world is fitted together by interchange between opposites, as are a lyre and a bow', and nothing in human life is pure and unalloyed. In music there are low notes and high notes, and in grammar there are vowels and consonants, and musicianship and literacy do not come from disliking and avoiding one or the other extreme, but from knowing how to make use of them all, and how to blend them into an appropriate mixture. Events too contain polarity: as Euripides says, 'Good and bad are inseparable, but blending is possible, to make things fine.' So, to continue our simile, we should not get discontented or give up when faced with discrepancy, but should behave like expert musicians: if someone plays bad music, they lessen its impact by playing better music, and they enclose wrong notes within right ones. So we should make our life's mixture harmonious and congruent with ourselves.

I mean, Menander is wrong when he says, 'From the moment of birth onwards, everyone is attended by a deity, who is an excellent guide through the mysteries of life.' Empedocles is more likely to be right with his view that each of us has two destinies or deities, which take us in hand and into their power when we are born: 'Earth was there, and far-seeing Sun, bloody Discord and tranquil Harmony, Beauty and Ugliness, Speed and Slowness, fair Truth and dark-locked Doubt.' Consequently, since at birth we admitted, all together, the potential for each of these experiences, and since we therefore inherently contain plenty of inconsistencies, anyone with any sense prays for the better things, but expects the others as well, and copes with both sets by never behaving excessively. For, in the first place, as Epicurus says, 'Increased pleasure in approaching the future depends on decreased need of it'; and in the second place, increased enjoyment of wealth, fame, power and status depends on decreased dread of their opposites, in the sense that a strong desire for each of them instils a very strong fear of their departure, and so weakens and destabilizes the pleasure, as if it were a candle flame in a draught. Anyone whom rationality allows to stand up to fortune fearlessly and unflinchingly, and say, 'You are welcome if you bring a gift, and no great ordeal if you leave', is enabled by his courage and fearlessness (because he knows that its departure would not be unbearable) thoroughly to enjoy whatever his present situation is. When Anaxagoras' son died, he declared, 'I knew that I had fathered a mortal'; and it is possible not to stop at admiring his character, which enabled him to say this, but also to mirror him by saying, whenever fortune intrudes, 'I know that the wealth I have is transitory and unstable'; 'I know that I owe my position to people who have the power to remove it'; 'I know that although my wife is good, she is a woman, and that my friend is human – a member of an inherently inconstant species, as Plato remarked.'

The point is that, if anything happens which may be unwelcome, but is not unexpected, this kind of preparedness and character leaves no room for 'I couldn't have imagined it' and 'This isn't what I'd hoped for' and 'I didn't expect this', and so stops the heart lurching and beating fast and so on, and quickly settles derangement and disturbance back on to a foundation. Carneades used to remind people who were involved in important affairs that unexpectedness is the be-all and end-all of distress and discontent. Consider, for example, how much smaller the Macedonian kingdom was than the Roman empire. Nevertheless, when Perseus lost Macedonia, not only did he complain bitterly about his own destiny, but it was universally held that his misfortune and fate were worse than absolutely everyone else's; but when Aemilius (who had defeated Perseus) resigned from his position of controlling more or less all the lands and seas in the world, he was fêted and he performed sacrifices to the gods for his acknowledged happiness. There was a good reason for this: Aemilius had accepted a position knowing that he would one day pass it on, whereas Perseus had lost his position unexpectedly. Homer too makes some good points about what happens when things are unexpected: Odysseus wept when his dog greeted him, but sat down impassively next to his sobbing wife; the reason is that he reached his wife with his emotions tamed and controlled by rational foresight, but he fell into the other situation without anticipating it – its surprising nature made it come out of the blue.

To express the matter generally, while some unwelcome events do by their very nature entail distress and pain, nevertheless, where the majority of such events are concerned, it is our minds that condition and teach us to resent them. Therefore, when faced with this latter category of unwelcome events, it is useful always to have available Menander's line, which says, 'No experience is terrible unless you make it so.' He is implicitly asking the question: Unless your body or mind are actually affected, what difference does it make to you if, for example, your father was not an aristocrat, your wife is having an affair, you fail to win some prize or you lose your right to the front seats in the theatre? For these occurrences do not stop a man being in excellent physical or mental condition. And where the former events are concerned, the ones which do seem by their very nature to cause distress – such as illness, stress and a friend's or child's death – then there is Euripides' famous line: 'I say "Poor me!"' – but why? I am only experiencing what it is to be human.' You see, no rational argument checks the downward slide of our emotions as well as one which reminds us that, in common with others and thanks to our nature, there are things which we cannot avoid; this necessity, which is due to corporeality, affords fortune its only hold on human beings; but corporeality is just one part of man's mixed nature, and in his most authoritative and important aspects he remains secure and stable.

When Demetrius had captured Megara, he asked Stilpo whether anything of his had been looted; Stilpo replied that he had seen nothing being carried off about which he would want to say 'mine'. So, if fortune steals and removes from us everything else, we still have something in us which is such that 'the Achaeans cannot carry or take it away'. It follows that we should not completely belittle and denigrate our nature as being weak, unstable and entirely subject to fortune; on the contrary, we know that the part of man which is flawed and unsound (and so liable to fortune) is small, and that we ourselves control the better part, which safely contains the most important of our benefits – correct beliefs, things we have learned and arguments conducive to goodness – which therefore subsist indelibly and indestructibly. If we are aware of this, the future doesn't dismay or terrify us and, where fortune is concerned, we say what Socrates said to the jurors (though he was apparently addressing his prosecutors) – that Anytus and Meletus can kill him, but not harm him.

The point is that fortune can make us fall ill, can deprive us of our wealth, can ruin our relationship with the people or the king, but it cannot make someone who is good, brave and high-minded into a bad, cowardly, mean-spirited, petty and spiteful person, and it cannot deprive us of the permanent presence of an attitude towards life which is a more helpful guide in this sphere than a helmsman is on a sea voyage. A helmsman is incapable of quelling a rough sea or the wind, and he cannot at will happen upon a safe harbour when he needs one, and he cannot endure whatever happens confidently and without flinching: as long as he doesn't give up, and relies on his skill, 'he escapes the hell-dark sea by reefing the mainsail right down to the bottom of the mast', but when the waves loom over him, he sits there quaking and trembling. On the other hand, a wise person's attitude calms the majority of physical matters, since his self-control, responsible regimen and moderate exercise get rid of the preconditions of illness; and if some external source of infection crops up, like the onset of a squall, then, in Asclepiades' words, 'he furls and lightens the sail, and rides it out'; and if some major unpredictable event overtakes and overwhelms him, the harbour is close by – he can swim away from the uncaulked hull of his body.

You see, it is not desire for life, but fear of death which makes an unintelligent person depend on his body and grasp on to it (one is reminded of how Odysseus' fear of Charybdis below him made him grasp on to the fig tree), 'when winds make both stopping and sailing impossible', and he is dissatisfied with one option and afraid of the other. However, anyone who has come, by whatever route, to understand the nature of the mind, and who appreciates that at death the change the mind undergoes is either for the better or at least not for the worse, is well equipped by this lack of fear of death to be content about his life. Anyone who can not only enjoy life when the pleasant and congenial aspect of it is uppermost, but who, when faced with an excess of events which are antipathetic and incongruent with his nature, can also depart without fear and with the words, 'The god himself will free me, when *I* will it' – well, it is inconceivable that such a man could be annoyed or angry or upset by anything that happened to him.

Whoever it was who said, 'Fortune, I have made a pre-emptive strike against you, and I have deprived you of every single loophole', was not basing his confidence on bolts, locks and fortifications, but on principles and arguments which are available to anyone who wants them. And this kind of argument should not induce any degree of resignation or disbelief, but admiration, emulation, enthusiasm, and investigation and observation of oneself in relatively trivial circumstances, to prepare oneself for the more important matters, so that one does not avoid them or divert one's mind from attention to them or take refuge in excuses like 'That's probably the most difficult thing I'll ever come across.' For if the mind is self-indulgent, and takes the easiest courses all the time, and retreats from unwelcome matters to what maximizes its pleasure, the consequence is weakness and feebleness born of lack of exertion; but a mind which trains and strains itself to use rationality to conceive an image of illness and pain and exile will find that there is plenty of unreality, superficiality and unsoundness in the apparent problems and horrors each of them has to offer, as detailed rational argument demonstrates.

Nevertheless, even the line of Menander which goes 'It is impossible for anyone still living to say, "That won't happen to me"' produces a shiver of fear in many people; but this is because they are unaware to what extent distress can be avoided by the beneficial practice of training oneself to gain the ability to look straight at fortune with open eyes, and not to form in oneself images which are 'soft and unweathered', like someone who has been brought up away from sunlight, in the shade of numerous hopes which constantly give way and provide no resistance against anything. However, we can also say the same thing as Menander – 'It is impossible for anyone still living to say, "That won't happen to me"' – but add that it is possible for anyone still living to say, 'Here's what I will not do: I will not lie, I will not mislead, I will not steal, I will not intrigue.' For this lies ready to hand, within our power, and its contribution towards contentment is not inconsiderable, but huge, since the alternative is for 'the realization of knowing that I have committed crimes' to mark the mind with remorse, which continually bleeds and stings like a bodily wound.

You see, while all other discomforts are eradicated by reason, it is reason itself which creates remorse, when the mind with its conscience is pricked and punished by itself. People who shiver from a chill or feel hot from a fever are more troubled and worse off than people who have the same sensations because of external heat or cold; likewise, chance events entail distress which is easier to endure, because it comes from an external source; but when 'What has happened to me is no one else's fault but my own' is the lament over one's mistakes, then because it comes from an internal source, from oneself, the result is a pain which one's sense of shame makes harder to bear. This is why a magnificent house, massive wealth, a splendid genealogy and high office, eloquence and fluency, are all incapable of giving life the degree of fair and calm weather that is afforded by a mind which is untainted by bad actions and intentions, and which bases life on a character that is calm and clear. A character like this is a fountain-head of fine achievements which entail not only present activity that is exuberant and happy and a source of pride, but also past memories that are more rewarding and secure than hopes which, as Pindar says, 'sustain one in old age'. Carneades said, 'Even if thuribles have been cleared out, they emit their scent for a long time.' And is it not the case that fine deeds leave behind in an intelligent person's mind an impression which remains pleasant and fresh, and thanks to which happiness is irrigated and thrives and he is enabled to rise above the level of those who moan and complain about life as being a vale of tears or a place designated for our soul's exile down here?

I like Diogenes' quip: once when he was visiting Sparta, he saw his host zealously getting ready for a festival day, and he said, 'Isn't it the mark of a good man to regard every day as a festival day?' And a particularly glorious festival too, if we see things aright. The world is a temple of the highest sacredness, and nowhere could be more suitable for divinity; and man is introduced into

this world by means of his birth not to view manufac-
tured, immobile images, but to gaze upon what Plato
describes as the perceptible likenesses of intelligible
things which divine intelligence has manifested as con-
tainers of an inherent principle of life and movement –
the sun, moon and stars, the rivers with their continuous
discharge of renewed water, and the earth with its supply
of means of nourishment for plants and creatures. Life
is an initiation into these things and there is no more
perfect way to celebrate them; life, therefore, should be
full of contentment and joy, and we should not make
the usual mistake of waiting for occasional days like
the holidays sacred to Cronus, Zeus or Athena for the
opportunity to enjoy and revivify ourselves by paying
mimes and dancers for bought entertainment.

Moreover, although we sit quietly and in good order
on these occasions – for no one complains while he is
being initiated or whinges while he is watching the
Pythian Games or is drinking during the festival of
Cronus – nevertheless, people bring shame on the festi-
vals, which are arranged and conducted by God, by
spending most of the rest of their time in complaints,
despondency and exhausting worry. And although
people enjoy listening to the delightful sounds of musical
instruments and the singing of birds, and enjoy watching
the play and frolics of animals, and conversely get perturbed when they growl and roar and look threaten-
ing, nevertheless when they see that their own lives
are unsmiling, depressed and constantly constrained and
restricted by disagreeable experiences and events and
innumerable anxieties, they are unwilling to find some

means of supplying themselves with recuperation and relaxation. But even when other people try to assist, they resist any argument which could help them come to terms with their current situation without finding fault with it, remember the past without ingratitude and approach the future happily and optimistically, without fear and without apprehension.